Alternative Weddings

A PRACTICAL GUIDE

Kate Gordon

ROBINSON
London

Constable & Robinson Ltd
3 The Lanchesters
162 Fulham Palace Road
London W6 9ER
www.constablerobinson.com

First published in the UK by Constable & Co. Ltd, 1998

This revised and updated edition published by Robinson,
an imprint of Constable & Robinson Ltd, 2002

A copy of the British Cataloguing in
Publication Data is available from the British Library.

ISBN 1-84119-606-1

Printed and bound in the EU

Contents

Acknowledgments

The following people have given me a great deal of advice and support in the compilation of this book and I am extremely grateful for their time and effort, so willingly given. The Rev. Canon Hill (Church of England); Rev. Peter Bell (CONCORD, Leeds); Annie Wildwood (Dragonpaths); Haviland Nye (British Buddhist Association); Robert Asby (executive director of the British Humanist Association); Anne Hosking (at the Religious Society of Friends); Marlena Schmool and Melna Charin (Board of Deputies of British Jews); Rev. Peter Norton (Appleby Parish Church); Rev. John Clifford (General Assembly of Unitarian and Free Christian Churches), David Whitfield, Superintendent Registrar, Penrith and District Register Office and the staff at the Registrar General's office. To the staff of Penrith Library who obtained a lot of my research material, to my agent Richard Gollner for his sensible advice and my editor Carol O'Brien and the staff at Constable Publishers. To Zoe Pilling and Kev Taylor, Peta and Ian, Rosie and Martin, Kirsty and Charlie, Clare and Alan, Rachel Barenblat, Aline, Kate and Stephen, Lynda, Ravi, Sharu, Tess and all the people who talked to me and shared their experiences freely but who did not want to be identified in print.

Thanks to Macmillan General Books for permission to quote from *The Collected Poems and Plays* by Rabindranath Tagore; to Random House for permission to quote from *A Gift from the Sea* by Anne Morrow Lindbergh; the British Humanist Association for permission to quote from *Sharing the Future*; Philip Carr-Gomm for permission to quote from his book *The Druid Way*; Sheil Land and Associates Ltd for permission to quote from James Roose-Evans' book *Passages of the Soul* and Dr John Boswell, *The Marriage of Likeness* published by HarperCollins; Victor Gollancz for permission to quote from *The Experience of Childbirth* by Sheila Kitzinger; Rev. Clare Edwards for material from *Human Rites*; Piatkus Books for permission to quote from Lorna St Aubyn's *Rituals for Everyday Living*; Routledge for permission to quote from *An Image Darkly Forming* by Bani Shorter, and Simone Weil, *Waiting For God*; HarperCollins for quotations from Madeleine L'Engle, *The Irrational Season*, and Kuan Tao Sheng's poem 'Married Love'; Faber and Faber for permission to quote Edwin Muir's poem 'The Confirmation'; artist Juliet Levy for permission to reproduce an illuminated Jewish marriage contract; words from *The Prophet* by Kahlil

Gibran are used by permission of the National Committee of Gibran, all rights reserved; the Central Board of Finance of the Church of England for permission to quote from the liturgy; extracts from the *Book of Common Prayer*, the rights in which are vested in the Crown, are reproduced by permission of the Crown's Patentee, Cambridge University Press. Every effort has been made by the author to trace copyright holders. The author and publishers would be pleased to hear from anyone whose name has been omitted due to incorrect information.

Introduction

How but in custom and in ceremony
Are innocence and beauty born?

W. B. YEATS

Committing yourself to a lifelong relationship with another person is one of the most solemn undertakings you can make, and it should also be the most joyful. Getting married in Britain used to mean either a standard church service or register office wedding that often made couples feel they were on an assembly line. The format was inflexible and difficult to adapt to individual circumstances. If the traditional religious ceremonies didn't fit your own beliefs the only alternative was a civil ceremony – usually held in dreary surroundings and so brief it felt meaningless. It was virtually impossible to have something personal, in fact any alternative was almost unheard of, as I found through my own experience.

1

Introduction

When I got married for the first time, it was a bleak register office ceremony followed by a church blessing to please our parents. We wanted to do something different, but the options didn't seem to be there – everything was dictated by convention or family politics. Although this relationship failed, we met again a few years later and decided to try again. We invited close friends and family for a big party, lit a candle and ceremonially burnt the decree nisi before exchanging rings and renewing our vows. It felt much more 'real' than our first wedding. This second attempt failed too and I now live with a new partner and the five children from our previous relationships. We periodically discuss making a formal commitment and the form it might take, but haven't made any decision yet. He talks of a jazz wedding with a big party. I dream of an absolutely private moment in a stunning location – a beach at the Bay of Islands in New Zealand, or an isolated stone circle in northern Scotland – just my partner, myself, two witnesses and the universe. Changes made to the law in the last few years have made it possible to have a wedding in a variety of new locations, in ways which are dramatically different. For the first time you can have a wedding that is uniquely yours and be as daring as you like!

WHY HAVE A CEREMONY AT ALL?

Although many more people now choose to live together without getting married, most people still opt for marriage at some time in their lives. It is the most important rite of passage we will ever celebrate, affecting our legal and financial status as well as our relationships with everyone around us. There is also an increasing trend for commitment ceremonies, which have no legal status, but all the emotional and psychological force of conventional rituals. Just because a union is not recognized by law doesn't make it any less valid – marriage has been regulated by law in England only since 1753, and in Scotland marriages 'by cohabitation' are still recognized as they always have been.

Why we should need any kind of public commitment at all is one of the questions I set out to answer when I wrote this book. Human beings seem to have a deep need for ceremony that goes far beyond mere social conditioning and has little to do with religious belief. Rites and rituals seem to be necessary to us, and it is a natural human instinct to celebrate the big events in our lives. For the Humanists, a ceremony 'is an opportunity to stand back and consider the step you are taking . . . to affirm and consolidate a personal commitment; to celebrate a life . . . or an event; to share feelings; and to strengthen ties with family and friends'. For others, ceremonies symbolize the changing, but infinite, nature of the universe, reinforcing 'our ability to cope with an unpredictable world. They heighten the intensity of shared experience, enabling us to realise that we are not alone but part of an indivisible whole.'[1]

Most of our ceremonies have very ancient origins and people are often unaware how much of the content is an amalgamation of ritual and symbolism from many different cultures and religions. We are now, also, a multicultural community; large sectors of the population belong to religions whose rites are not understood by the majority. It is important to respect each other's ceremonies. There is a growing diversity of belief in British society. While Christian churches are being turned into blocks of flats and arts centres as their congregations dwindle, mosques and Hindu temples are being built all over the country. There are Buddhist centres in most big towns and the New Age pagan, once regarded as 'fringe', is now part of the mainstream. At the same time, increasing numbers of people see religion of any kind as ethnically divisive, untruthful and an extension of society's attempts to control the life of an individual.

The result of this is that people of every race, creed and class are marrying each other, producing a blending of cultures and beliefs which hasn't been seen in Britain since the Saxon, Viking and Romano-British cultures came together around AD 500. There has never been a greater need for ceremonies that are flexible and personal, to fit what should be a unique occasion.

In this book I have tried to give a brief outline of the

[1] James Roose-Evans, *Passages of the Soul.*

law, a guide to the basic religious ceremonies, indications as to how they can be adapted and personalized as well as a full account of the alternatives for the increasing number of people who do not practise any kind of religion.

Marriage

Pussy said to the Owl 'You elegant fowl!
How charmingly sweet you sing.
O let us be married! Too long we have tarried;
But what shall we do for a ring?'

EDWARD LEAR

Marriage is popular because it combines the maximum
of temptation with the maximum of opportunity.

GEORGE BERNARD SHAW

The history of marriage is intriguing and very far from the modern romantic notions we have of love and commitment. In Roman or Greek times, and in Europe until relatively recently, marriage was largely about property and the rearing of children. Marriages were generally arranged but, contrary to expectations, often ended in deep affection. In complete contrast, modern marriage is usually entered in deep affection or romantic love, becomes centred in mid-life around property and the rearing of children, and ends – three or four times out of ten – in acrimony and divorce.

In the days when women had no separate legal identity of their own, they were the property of their fathers and then their husbands. Any money or real estate they were entitled to also became the property of their male relatives. When a woman was given in marriage, it meant exactly that; she was considered as property to be transferred from one adult male to another. A marriage contract was a property contract. Many of the words of the modern marriage ceremony – for example 'to have and to hold, from this time forward' – come from the standard Roman form of contract.

In the early Christian church in Britain, marriage remained a civil business and it was only after the thirteenth century that it became a sacrament, requiring the offices of a priest. From the thirteenth century onwards, a whole body of church law evolved to regulate personal relationships – the legality of marriages and the paternity of offspring having a direct bearing on the transfer and inheritance of land and property. This really affected only the property-owning classes – the poor continued to make 'common-law' commitments as they had always done, with or without the blessing of the church. In Scotland, such relationships are still recognized in law as 'a marriage by cohabitation with habit and repute'. Modern English marriage law dates from Hardwicke's Marriage Act in 1753 with further revisions made in the nineteenth century.

The patriarchal nature of the traditional marriage ceremony, and its emphasis on child-bearing, has been a cause of concern to both men and women for a long time. The wording of the Christian marriage ceremony and the injustice of the marriage laws in England were regarded by the reformer Robert Owen as 'the barbarous relics of a feudal, despotic system' in a speech he made before his own wedding in 1832, and a nineteenth-century American feminist, Lucy Stone, stood up with her husband at her wedding ceremony and made the following declaration, which might well find resonances with twenty-first century feminists! 'While we acknowledge our mutual affection by publicly assuming the relationship of husband and wife ... we deem it a duty to declare that this act on our part implies no sanction of, nor promise of voluntary obedience to such of the present laws of marriage as refuse to recognize the wife as an independent, rational being, while they confer upon the husband an injurious and unnatural superiority . . .'

Modern marriage is a ceremony that celebrates the desire of two people to commit themselves to each other for life. They need a ritual that will reflect their beliefs and personality as honestly as possible. It should be a joyful, loving celebration of personal commitment, the exchange of promises in front of chosen friends and family in a sympathetic setting. For most people, a public, formal commitment, using the ancient, solemn concept of the vow, is far more meaningful than a purely private promise which can be made on the spur of an emotional moment. A formal ceremony also changes the way that the other people view their relationship. Marriage still carries more weight socially and psychologically than mere cohabitation.

There are two elements to the marriage ceremony – the legal contract recognized by the state and the exchange of vows. The legal element consists of a declaration made in a certain form of words in front of a registrar and two independent witnesses, followed by the signing of the certificate. Your signature on the marriage certificate is just as binding as your signature on any other type of contract. Church of England ministers have the same status as registrars and so a church wedding will satisfy the full legal requirements – as do both Quaker and Jewish weddings. But less than half of all marriages now take place in a religious building and there is an increasing trend towards separating the legal aspect of the ceremony from the celebration and commitment side and a tremendous surge in the demand for a purely civil ceremony.

As most marriages today involve the joint ownership of property, many couples now draw up pre-nuptial agreements, which are increasingly recognized by the courts. Couples who decide to live together without marrying, or have a wedding ceremony that is not recognized by the state, can have a cohabitation contract drawn up by a lawyer. Although it may seem cynical, this makes good sense, and can save a lot of argument if things go wrong. But it is also important to note that if circumstances change dramatically, or there are children, or the relationship has lasted for a long time, the courts may choose to ignore the agreement if they regard it as grossly unfair to either party.

Opting for a civil marriage in front of a registrar, which deals with the legal and contractual side of things, gives a couple who want a non-traditional ceremony the freedom to choose. Your marriage ceremony can then be conducted in your own special way, according to your own beliefs and in a place of your own choosing, free from the rules and regulations that surround more traditional rites – and it can still be a religious ceremony if you wish. In almost every other country in Europe a two-part wedding is the norm – a short civil ceremony at the town hall followed by the 'real' marriage either in church, in a private chapel or at home.

INTER-FAITH MARRIAGE

Religion and culture are often so closely entwined that marrying someone who has been brought up with a different religious background can bring many problems. At one level it symbolizes social integration and greater unity, but at another level it can bring a sense of grief as well as fears of a loss of cultural identity. Family and friends may also worry about the couple's future life together in the face of what may seem irreconcilable differences. Rachel Barenblat, a young American academic, writes that 'As a Jewish woman engaged to a non-Jewish man, I'm intimately familiar with the particular joys and difficulties of an inter-faith relationship. They're indescribable, and I sense they're slightly different for each couple, depending on each couple's relationship to their parents and families, to the religions and cultures in which they were reared, to God, to each other. I have my own personal ways of dealing with this stuff;

I cry, I write letters home that I never send, I laugh, I bake bread, I write poems, I read books on the subject, and I have long intense talks with my partner late at night.' In extreme cases, marrying out of the faith may also mean marrying out of the family and the community.

Different faiths have different attitudes towards inter-faith marriage. Orthodox Jews will not countenance it; the Catholic Church will allow marriage to other Christians by dispensation; Muslims will expect non-Muslims to convert; Buddhists and Hindus are very tolerant of the beliefs of others and marriage is not regarded as a sacrament. But there is a growing movement towards tolerance as society becomes more and more multi-cultural, and several organizations exist to promote a more genuinely ecumenical approach. There are now an increasing number of ordained Interfaith ministers, representatives from many different religions, specially trained to conduct inter-faith marriages and give spiritual counselling. (see Useful Addresses for contact details.)

Many couples who belong to different faiths please their families by having two weddings. Noor, a science graduate, whose Muslim parents moved to London from Lahore when she was small, met and fell in love with Paul – an English Christian – at university. She had always accepted that she would have to have an arranged marriage, though her parents were willing to wait until she was ready. Noor kept her relationship secret for three years, even though she was living with Paul for two of them. Eventually, supported by her brother, she told her parents that she wanted to marry Paul. Although initially they were shocked, they recognized that her feelings were not going to change, and when they met Paul they found that they really liked him. Paul agreed to make a nominal conversion to Islam to please Noor's parents, and, as well as an Islamic marriage ceremony, they also had a civil wedding in a hotel with the traditional white dress (which Noor confessed she had always coveted!) for Paul's family. Noor's brother Ahmed was best man at the civil ceremony, and two of Noor's English girl friends from university donned saris and became her 'bridesmaids' for the Islamic marriage. Noor was delighted that the compromise succeeded in bringing the families together. 'It worked much better than I ever hoped it could, and I'm still ecstatically happy.'

THE LAW

You can't marry in Britain if you are under sixteen. If you are between sixteen and eighteen (unless you live in Scotland) you need parental consent. At any age you must be single, widowed or legally divorced (this means a decree absolute), of different sexes, and you must not be within the legally prohibited degrees of relationship – i.e. parent/child, brother/sister, or close blood relatives other than cousins. Failure to meet any of these criteria renders the marriage void. Marriages which have taken place abroad where the legal age is lower than in Britain are recognized here if the couple subsequently move to Britain, but in cases where under-age British citizens have been taken abroad to be married, the courts have usually declared the marriage null and void.

The law controls where and how you can be married. People wishing to be married have the choice of a religious ceremony according to their own beliefs, or a civil ceremony. In many cases it is necessary to have both, since the rites of some religious denominations are not recognized in English law. However, an increasing number of premises are registered for both worship and marriage – including mosques and Sikh temples – and, providing the ceremony is conducted by the 'authorized person' specified in the registration certificate, there will be no need for a separate ceremony.

A civil ceremony can take place in a register office or, under the new marriage laws, in licensed premises which can include hotels, stately homes, castles, moored boats or function suites in football stadiums and cricket clubs. The venue must be licensed and a registrar present. The Registrar General has a directory of licensed venues which you can buy (see Useful Publications) and your local register office should be able to tell you what is available in your area. The only stipulation for obtaining a licence for premises is that they must be fixed (i.e. not mobile), open to the public, suitably solemn and indoors. You could apply to have a venue licensed yourself if you were willing to pay the fee – this varies from district to district but is currently about £750. Your own home is unlikely to be granted a licence unless it is already a public building. There is a further stipulation that the ceremony should not take place in a room where people are going to eat within an hour.

In any other location – such as a deconsecrated church, a stone circle, your garden, or any other outdoor setting – ministers of the Unitarian Church, retired or 'freelance' clergy, Humanist or New Age celebrants are usually willing to conduct a ceremony, but a separate civil ceremony in front of a registrar must also take place.

In Scotland the law is different and it is the celebrant who is licensed, not the premises. So, you can get married anywhere – on a beach, under a waterfall, in your own garden or a chapel or hotel, even in a hot-air balloon, in a malt whisky distillery or up a mountain, providing that the celebrant is willing to officiate. And, as generations of Gretna Green elopers have discovered, it isn't necessary to live in Scotland to have a Scottish wedding.

There are certain exemptions from the requirements of the law for people who are seriously ill, housebound, in prison or sectioned under the Mental Health Act. For those who are terminally ill, it is possible to get a Registrar General's licence – valid for a month – which will enable a marriage to take place at any time and at any venue specified in the application. All that is needed is a letter from a doctor confirming that the patient is terminally ill, cannot be moved to a registered venue, is capable of understanding the nature of the ceremony and consenting to it, and that the signatory is the patient's own doctor. It is then possible to be married in a hospice, hospital ward or even your own home. A similar licence can be obtained by those who are housebound or detained in an institution for at least three months, giving permission to be married there.

GETTING MARRIED ABROAD

If you want to have a wedding on a tropical island or in any other foreign location, there are a number of holiday companies who will provide a package for you. Alternatively you can arrange it yourself. If you want to get married in France, Rumania, Greece or any other foreign country you will have to comply with the marriage laws of that country including residence qualifications. The appropriate embassy should be able to tell you what the requirements are. You will probably need your birth certificates, a certificate of no-impediment (obtained from your local register office), passports, decree absolute (if applicable), proof of employment in the UK, and the hire of a translator for the ceremony. In some European countries the procedure is easier than it is in Britain, but in others, such as Italy, there is a longer residence qualification. Make sure that you arrange it all well in advance – things take longer when they have to be done from a distance. A friend who wanted to get married in Prague needed several months to make the necessary arrangements, but the resulting civil ceremony, conducted in both English and Czech, was much more friendly and meaningful than its English equivalent.

If it's your ambition to get married in Las Vegas, then

all you need to do is take with you your birth certificates, passports and decree absolute (if you've been married and divorced), and death certificate of previous spouse if widowed. The wedding can be arranged at a few hours' notice simply by making a phone call from the hotel, but advance booking at any of the many wedding chapels can be arranged if you wish. They will offer a number of alternative packages from a simple ceremony to a complete formal wedding service with dress and veil, flowers, music, limousine, minister, photographer – and matching T-shirts to commemorate the event! Most American states require couples to take a blood test before the wedding.

Hawaii is also becoming a popular American destination for marriage. Several travel companies offer a package, but if you want to do it yourself, enquire about the legal requirements from the United States Embassy before you go. If you really want a tropical island wedding, and Hawaii and the Seychelles are too far away, think about the Caribbean. Most of the Caribbean islands have a short residence qualification, and you can be married there after a stay of only two or three days.

If you would like to be married on skis, Virgin Snow Weddings offer packages to Vermont and Nevada. There are several options including marriage in a wedding chapel, at the Nevada Casino, in the Olde England Inne, on the shores of Lake Tahoe – or you can ask the Official Notary to marry you on the ski-slope itself! An added bonus is that Vermont and Nevada do not require couples to have blood tests.

Some couples dream of being married on a ship at sea by the captain, but this is no longer possible as a legal option. Many cruise companies, such as Cunard, will arrange for a ceremony of 'blessing or commitment' to take place on board ship, conducted by the captain, complete with champagne and party afterwards, but they stress that it will not be legal unless the couple have already had a civil ceremony in accordance with English law. They also arrange ceremonies for the renewal of vows. It is possible to be legally married on a cruise liner in American waters, provided that the ship is tied up in dock at the time, and many of the shipping companies operating from ports in the USA can offer this as an option.

Australia and New Zealand have become very popular destinations for marriage – not least because the weather is reliably warm and proceedings are conducted in English. Both countries have extensive civil celebrancy programmes, where trained, licensed celebrants can conduct ceremonies in any location and with any suitable form of words the couple want. Official Notice of Intention to Marry must be given to the chosen celebrant at least a month before the marriage ceremony. This can be done over the internet. Legal details, the Notice itself and lists of celebrants can be found on the internet: for Australia at **www.netspace.net.au/ ~afcc/Pages/MarriageLegal.htm** and New Zealand at **www.bdm.govt.nz/diawebsite.nsf/**

Marriages which take place abroad in ways which are not legal in this country are recognized providing they were legally valid in the place where they were solemnized. They will only be deemed to be void here if the parties were British citizens and either under-age, already married, the same sex, or closely related.

EXOTIC LOCATIONS

You can have a wedding ceremony in a hot-air balloon, underwater, on top of a mountain, sky-diving, on a beach, in a woodland glade, in a stone circle, on top of a number 28 bus or on boats, trains or planes – so long as you are aware that, in England, Wales and Northern Ireland, you will need a separate civil ceremony to make it fully legal. In Scotland all you need is a celebrant willing to marry you, and to ensure that the location you choose is stationary at the time of the ceremony. Among a multitude of available public sites, it is possible to get married on the top of Ben Nevis, in a riverside grotto on the River Tay at Stakis Dunkeld House or by the Grey Mare's Tail, a spectacular waterfall owned by the National Trust for Scotland. There are dozens of stone circles and miles and miles of wonderful coastline. If you're a whisky connoisseur, you can also get married in the Glenturret Malt Whisky Distillery in Perthshire! Both the National Trust for Scotland and Historic Scotland can provide full details of properties available for wedding ceremonies.

VIRTUAL WEDDINGS

Getting married in cyberspace could be fun! Virtual marriage is currently being pioneered in America, complete with headsets and a huge screen for the invited guests. There's nothing to stop you exchanging vows by e-mail or even online, but it won't be legal in Britain unless you do the civil bit as well!

RELIGIOUS CEREMONIES

The Anglican Church is one of the few religious bodies in Britain that can legally marry people – clergy are also registrars. Under current law, theoretically you can choose the day you want the marriage to take place, but remember that the vicar has the right to choose the time, so if you insist on an inconvenient date such as Christmas Eve, he may well schedule the ceremony very early in the morning!

A church wedding is only legal if it takes place during the day and with open doors – a historical anomaly to prevent clandestine marriages! To be married in a church you will probably need to fulfil the residence qualifications for that parish – usually a minimum of three weeks and sometimes as much as six months. Marriage is either by notice and banns or by common licence, providing the residence qualifications have been fulfilled. Notice and banns means that the names of the couple to be married will be read out in church for three consecutive Sundays before the marriage in the parishes of both the bride and groom. Historically this was to give members of the community the chance to object. Common licence avoids the necessity of reading banns. In certain circumstances a special licence may be granted allowing a couple to marry at any time and at a church of their choice. This is sometimes granted where the couple have a particular attachment to a church outside their own parish, or where they want to avoid unwelcome publicity, or need to be married quickly.

As the Church of England is the established church of the state, this creates an obligation to marry any parishioner who asks, providing they satisfy all the residence and other criteria. However, the vicar is not obliged to conduct the ceremony personally and can refuse to marry someone living within the parish if he feels that the couple do not have the necessary religious commitment. They will then have to find another clergyman willing to conduct the marriage, possibly a retired vicar, or one of the new 'freelance' clergymen (see Useful Addresses). There are many who have a more liberal approach. One clergyman was approached by two Sikhs who lived within the parish, asking to be married. Although he suspected that their motives were other than religious, he agreed to marry them in accordance with his own ecumenical beliefs although he knew that it was likely to be the only time they would ever enter a Christian church. If one partner has been divorced it may be very difficult to find a clergyman willing to conduct the ceremony, unless the divorced partner has since died. But officially the church has no ruling on remarriage of divorcees at the moment – practice varies from diocese to diocese and much will depend on the views held by the individual clergyman.

For any other Christian denomination (except for Quakers) and members of other faiths (except for Jews), notice of marriage must be given to the Registrar of Births, Marriages and Deaths in the district where either partner lives. A registrar must be present at the service or there must be a separate civil ceremony. A limited number of mosques and chapels may be registered for marriages and have an 'authorized person' (in effect a registrar) to conduct the ceremony. Jews and Quakers have always been exempt from these restrictions and their ceremonies can take place at any time of day, indoors or outdoors, and still be valid.

Each religious denomination has its own basic form of service – how much couples are permitted to alter or personalize the ceremony varies a great deal. In the case of a civil ceremony, there are certain words that must be spoken, but otherwise the content of the service is negotiable between the individuals and the registrar provided it is restricted to non-religious material.

The greatest element of freedom is obtained by having a short civil ceremony to cover the legal requirements and then to design your own wedding service to be held in the place of your choice, whether licensed or not – conducted by the person of your choice. This can be religious or secular, Christian, Humanist, Pagan,

Buddhist, Muslim, Hindu or Jewish or a blend of all of them.

It may be helpful to talk to an ordained Interfaith minister about the content of the ceremony and its implications. Details can be found on **www.interfaithministers. org.uk**

If you are divorced and unable to remarry in church but still want a religious ceremony there are a number of options. A civil ceremony followed by a service of blessing in your usual place of worship is the most popular. These services are very flexible in content and a sympathetic minister or priest will encourage you to make it as personal and meaningful as possible. And, since there is no legal element involved in a service of blessing, it can be held in any location you choose, including your own garden, a beach, or a hotel.

Alternatively there are several denominations which recognize the frailty of human relationships. Your local Free Church minister may be willing to marry you in these circumstances. Methodists, Baptists, the United Reformed Church, and Quakers all allow remarriage. This list includes the Unitarian Church, which has an extremely liberal outlook. Unitarians believe that God is one person, not three, and that Jesus Christ was not divine, but an exceptional human being whose teachings are to be revered. There is no set liturgy, and Unitarian ministers (many of whom are also 'authorized persons') will construct a wedding ceremony that is wholly individual to the couple concerned, although to comply with the law it must include the basic form of words outlined below. Readings and prayers can be included from other religious traditions – something which can be invaluable in the case of the mixed-faith marriage. The ceremony can take place in a church or other licensed premises, or anywhere in Scotland. Some Unitarian ministers will also conduct 'ceremonies of commitment' for same-sex unions.

For those who have no particular faith, but want a ceremony with a high spiritual content, it is possible to have a Humanist ceremony. 'Humanists look on marriage as a commitment that involves mutual love and respect. Each party has a responsibility for the welfare of the other, and to the success of the relationship. Where the couple have children the commitment involves a shared responsibility for their well-being and development . . . The close and loving relationship of two human beings that is the central feature of marriage lies right at the heart of Humanism.' Humanist celebrants will also sometimes marry those whose unions are not recognized by British law, including transsexuals, lesbians and gays.

CIVIL CEREMONIES

If you are getting married in a register office or other licensed premises with a registrar present, the law will not allow you to incorporate into the ceremony any readings or music that have any religious associations whatsoever (this even includes Mendelssohn's Wedding March – though this originally came from *A Midsummer Night's*

Dream!). So readings from the Bible are out, as are sacred music and any poetry or other text that mentions God, or even 'the heavens'. This seems extremely unfair and bureaucratic, since it can have no bearing on the actual legality of the ceremony, and is even more of an argument for the European custom of having a brief civil ceremony first followed by your own form of rite where you are free to choose whatever you wish.

The law regulating marriage in a register office in England and Wales has recently been changed. The system of certificates and licences, including the special licence, has been abolished and replaced by a 'certificate of common notice'. Bride and groom are now required to have been resident in Britain for at least seven days before they give notice to be married. Notice of marriage must be given at least fifteen clear days before the marriage is to take place. Both bride and groom are required to give notice in person before the superintendent registrar in the area where they live. It is also necessary to provide proof of nationality – a passport, identity card or other approved document – and they may be asked to produce birth certificates and divorce documents if applicable. They will then be issued with a 'certificate of common notice' which is valid for up to twelve months. Further information can be obtained from the website of the General Register Office for England and Wales on **www.statistics.gov.uk/nsbase/registration/marriage.asp**

A white paper has recently proposed changes to the law which would licence registrars to conduct ceremonies in any location deemed 'suitable and appropriate'.

This would include your own home, and the venue would not need to be licensed – bringing English law into line with Scotland. However, even if the legislation is passed, it will not come into effect until 2004 at the earliest.

In Scotland, notice must be given to the registrar at least fifteen days (but not more than three months) before the marriage by the submission of two registration forms accompanied by the birth certificates of both parties, decree nisi, etc. You do not have to live in Scotland to be married in Scotland; the preliminaries can all be done by post. The Registration Office at Gretna Green (see Useful Addresses) provides an information pack which gives the details and this will be sent on receipt of an A4 self-addressed envelope stamped to the value of 70p. The Schedule of Marriage can then be collected in person, if necessary only ten minutes before the ceremony. If you are having a religious ceremony, or a civil ceremony at another location, the Schedule is given to the minister, or registrar, signed afterwards by the couple and taken back to the register office to be registered.

The Ceremony

The legal nucleus of the marriage ceremony in England, Wales and Northern Ireland – whether the ceremony is a religious or a civil one – is the requirement that the bride and groom should declare that they are free to marry and that they do indeed, of their own free will, agree to marry each other. They are then declared man and wife. Each person in turn will be asked to repeat the following form of words:

I do solemnly declare that I know not of any lawful impediment why I [name] may not be joined in matrimony to [name] . . .

I call upon these persons here present to witness that I [name] do take thee [name] to be my lawful wedded husband/wife . . .

ANGLICAN

Whenever marriage is mentioned, it is the words of the old form of service from the sixteenth-century prayer book that come to mind. However, the traditional ceremony, with its patriarchal notions of the woman being 'given' to the man by her father, and the promise to 'obey', has fallen into disuse. Since the 1960s most couples have opted either for a modified form, or for the Alternative Services Book which gives a modern language version. This ceremony has been superseded by another revision, which is already being used in many churches.

There have been changes in the customary format as well as in the wording. Bride and groom are free to walk down the aisle together if they wish. If the bride wants to be 'given away' she can be accompanied by her mother, or a relative or friend of either sex. Provision is made for the bride to give the bridegroom a ring and the promises made to each other are the same, reflecting the equality aspired to in contemporary relationships. Many people, however, still like the sheer poetry of the old form of service rather than the modern language version, even if they decide to omit the promise to obey.

The Book of Common Prayer 1552

Then shall the Priest say unto the Man: *Wilt thou have this Woman to thy wedded wife, to live together after God's ordinance in the Holy estate of Matrimony? Wilt thou love her, comfort her, honour, and keep her in sickness and in health: and, forsaking all other, keep thee only unto her, so long as ye both shall live?*

The Man shall answer: *I will.*

Then shall the Priest say unto the Woman: *Wilt thou have this Man to thy wedded husband, to live together after God's ordinance in the Holy estate of Matrimony? Wilt thou obey him, and serve him, love, honour, and keep him in sickness and in health; and, forsaking all other, keep thee only unto him, so long as ye both shall live?*

The Woman shall answer: *I will.*

[Then the couple turn to face each other, and the man takes the bride's right hand in his. Then the man repeats after the priest:]

I [name] take thee [name] to my wedded wife, to have and to hold from this day forward, for better for worse, for richer for poorer, in sickness and in health, to love and to cherish, till death us do part, according to God's holy ordinance: and thereto I plight thee my troth.

Then shall they loose their hands; and the Woman, with her right hand taking the Man by his right hand, shall likewise say after the Minister:

I [name] take thee [name] to my wedded husband, to have and to hold from this day forward, for better for worse, for richer for poorer, in sickness and in health, to love, cherish and to obey, till death us do part, according to God's holy ordinance: and thereto I give thee my troth.

[The priest blesses the ring. Then the man takes the ring from the priest and places it on the first, second and third fingers of the woman's left hand as each member of the Holy Trinity is named, leaving it upon the third finger.]

With this Ring I thee wed, with my body I thee worship, and with all my worldly goods I thee endow; In the Name of the Father, and of the Son, and of the Holy Ghost. Amen.

The new service currently proposed is much shorter than the original and the language is very simple and dignified. There is a short greeting to the guests, a prayer of preparation and an introduction which includes the following statement of Christian marriage.

The Scriptures teach us that marriage is a gift of God in creation and a means of his grace, a holy mystery in which man and woman become one flesh. It is God's purpose that, as husband and wife give themselves to each other in love throughout their lives, they shall be united in that love as Christ is united with his Church.

Marriage is given that husband and wife may comfort and help each other, living faithfully together in need and in plenty, in sorrow and in joy. It is given, that with delight and tenderness they may know each other in love, and, through the joy of their bodily union, may strengthen the union of their hearts and lives. It is given, that they may have children and be blessed in caring for them and bringing them up in accordance with God's will, to his praise and glory.

The wording of the declaration of intent is a simplified version of the early ceremony:

[Name] will you take [name] to be your wedded wife/ husband? Will you love her/him, comfort her/ him, honour and protect her/him, and, forsaking all others, be faithful to her/him as long as you both shall live?

So too are the vows:

I, [name] take you [name] to be my wedded husband/wife, to have and to hold from this day forward; for better, for worse, for richer, for poorer, in sickness and in health, to love and to cherish, till death us do part; according to God's holy law. All this I vow before God.

What is different is that family and friends are now included in the promises of commitment. The minister asks: *Will you, the family and friends of [name] and [name] support and uphold them in their marriage now and in the years to come?*

The vows are followed by an exchange of rings, readings, a sermon (or short address) and the blessing of the marriage. The ceremony can be extended to include communion if the couple wish, and hymns or other music can be included.

It is not generally permissible to alter the standard church liturgy, but very minor alterations to the form of service to make it more personal are allowed by some ministers. After discussion with the minister, you may be allowed to add in personal prayers, vows and readings at suitable moments. In the revised liturgy the vow to 'obey' and the giving away ceremony are omitted, and the parts of the service which are inappropriate for older couples beyond child-bearing age and for those who are unable to have children for other reasons are optional.

ROMAN CATHOLIC NUPTIAL MASS

'God who created man out of love also calls him to love.' Marriage is regarded as a sacrament in the Catholic Church; 'the intimate community of life and love which constitutes the married state has been established by the Creator and endowed by him with its own proper laws . . . God himself is the author of marriage.' It is regarded as the human parallel of Christ's marriage to the church. The health of the individual and of society in general is held to be directly linked to the sanctity of marriage and family life. Catholic marriage is indissoluble. This means that a civil divorce will not be recognized by the Catholic Church, although an annulment may be granted in certain circumstances. The annulment procedure is complex and almost always takes a long time to complete.

The wording of the Roman Catholic marriage service sprang from the same root as the liturgy of the Church of England, and differs only in small details. The ceremony usually includes communion, but only baptized Catholics will be able to receive the eucharist. If one of the partners is from another denomination or from another faith, the service will probably take an abbreviated form, rather than the full mass, and may require a dispensation.

Roman Catholic priests are not registrars, so a registrar may have to be present, unless the church has been licensed for marriages, in which case the priest becomes an 'authorized person'. There is also more form-filling for a Catholic marriage, since the priest must be satisfied that you have not been married before. The priest should be approached well in advance, so that all the necessary preparations can be made. Couples may also be asked to attend classes, so that they are aware of the responsibilities of Catholic marriage and parenthood.

How much you will be allowed to tailor the ceremony to your own wishes, and the music and readings you may have, depends on the individual priest.

At the heart of a Catholic marriage is the element of consent and free will. The couple must consent to take each other as husband and wife, without coercion or 'grave external fear'. If it can be proved that they were under any kind of external pressure that invalidated consent, there may later be grounds for annulment. Catholics who have had a civil divorce and have remarried are regarded by the Catholic Church as living in adulterous relationships and may be refused communion, though this is not always strictly applied.

FREE CHURCH DENOMINATIONS

With the exception of the Unitarians, who have no set liturgy, many of the Nonconformist churches have now adopted a ceremony very similar to the modern English

33

Anglican version. However, there is considerably more scope for customizing the service according to the needs of the individual couple. Readings, music, your own prayers and personal vows can be incorporated by discussion with the minister in charge. Some Nonconformist churches, such as the Methodists, are not against marrying people who have been divorced.

SERVICE OF BLESSING

If you want a religious ceremony and are unable to get married in church for whatever reason, a service of blessing following a civil ceremony is the next best thing. This can also be held in a hotel, or licensed building, if you are having your civil marriage there – or, if your minister is willing, in your own home, or an outdoor location.

One of the nicest blessings is one used by the Church of Scotland, to be found in the Common Order Book.

The couple enter together attended by their friends and family (bridesmaids, flower girls and groomsmen are quite appropriate). The minister welcomes everyone and there are prayers and readings before the minister makes the following statement:

We rejoice in the marriage of [name] and [name] and are happy to ask God to bless it.

[Name] and [name] have been married according to the law of the land. They have pledged their love and loyalty to

each other. Now, in faith, they come before God and his Church to acknowledge their covenant of marriage.

In Christian marriage, a man and a woman bind themselves to each other in love, and become one, even as Christ is one with the Church. They are committed to love each other as Christ loved the Church and gave himself for it.

Prayers are offered for the couple that they 'may keep the vows they have already made'. They then face each other, holding hands, and make the following promises:

[Name] you are my wife/husband. With God's help, I promise to be your faithful husband/wife, to love you as Christ commands, to comfort you and protect you, to honour you, as long as we both shall live.

The rings are blessed with the following words:

May the ring(s) you wear be a symbol of unending love and faithfulness, to remind you of the covenant into which you have entered.

There are prayers of blessing, and then the minister declares that the couple are indeed man and wife before God.

QUAKER

Quakers meet for worship without a liturgy or other planned words, without outward sacraments or pre-arranged actions, without a priest, wherever and whenever it is convenient. In a framework of silence, the Quakers wait for a deeper understanding and communion with God; a few of the worshippers may be inspired to speak, perhaps with their own words, a prayer or a reading. All Quaker meetings for worship in Britain follow this basic pattern.

Quaker marriages take place at a specially convened Meeting. There is no celebrant, just simple pledges by the couple in front of the Friends, specially invited guests and the Society of Friends' Registering Officer (most local areas have one). When the Meeting has settled into silent worship and when the couple feel ready, they stand and face each other and repeat these words:

Friends, I take this my friend [name] to be my wife/husband, promising, through divine assistance (or with God's help), to be unto her/him a loving and faithful husband/wife, so long as we both on earth shall live.

Rings aren't considered necessary, but may be exchanged by the couple. Another period of prayer and meditation follows during which Friends may be moved to pray aloud for the blessing of the couple. Quakers, like the Anglican Church, can register their own marriages.

A Quaker marriage certificate.
(© *Library of the Religious Society of Friends in Britain*)

A Quaker marriage certificate, signed by the couple and the first four witnesses, is read to the Friends by the registering officer during the course of the Meeting. Everyone present, including the smallest child, is also a witness. A civil marriage certificate, to be sent to the authorities, is then signed by the registering officer, the couple and two witnesses.

Non-members can be married under the care of a Quaker Meeting if their understanding of marriage is in sympathy with Quaker views and if the Meeting knows the couple well enough to offer friendship and pastoral care. Marriage of couples who have been divorced is not forbidden, if the couple are sincere in their commitment to each other and their desire for a religious ceremony to formalize their relationship. It is important to emphasize that a Quaker marriage is a Christian commitment and not a secular alternative.

UNITARIAN

Whereas many religious denominations view marriage as a holy sacrament, ordained by God, the Unitarian view of marriage is that 'the decision to marry is made by two individuals in relation to their communities and their own spiritual visions, rather than as an act of obedience and conformity to particular religious codes . . . the rite of marriage in a Unitarian place of worship has more to do with the desire of people to add a spiritual dimension to their freely chosen act.'

It is rare for anyone to be turned away; the Unitarians welcome people from different faiths and those who have been divorced, providing that the couple 'have thought seriously about their desire to be married' and their wish 'to celebrate it in a spiritual context'.

A Unitarian wedding ceremony is completely individual, although in England and Wales it must include the legal form of words. Otherwise the content and the format are arranged in discussion between the minister and the couple to be married, who will decide the style of language, readings, music and vows. The ceremony can include readings and prayers from a variety of different religious traditions.

In Scotland, Unitarian ministers can marry you at any time of day and almost any location you choose. In England and Wales, it must be during the hours of daylight and in a building registered for public worship and/or licensed for the solemnization of weddings. However, if you want a ceremony in your garden or any other exotic location in England or Wales, Unitarian ministers are happy to conduct it, providing the couple are aware that, for full legality, they need to have a separate civil marriage.

HUMANIST

The growing attraction of a Humanist ceremony has been summed up by Claire Rayner in a single paragraph. 'There are in Britain a great many thoughtful people who have ideals and aspirations that owe nothing to religious affiliation, who want to enter into committed marital relationships with a public ceremony to mark the rite of passage. But they feel uneasy at the thought of going through a religious one, which implies they have beliefs they do not in fact hold, or through a registrar's which offers no satisfying emotional or personal content.'

The Humanists now have a national network of trained officiants, and publish a booklet, *Sharing the Future*, which outlines their aims and offers sample ceremonies and readings. In it, Jane Wynne Wilson writes that: 'The Humanist concept of a wedding ceremony is quite distinctive. It illuminates important values and beliefs while giving expression to two people's personalities. Moreover, there is a flexibility and openness of approach that is quite unusual. Remarriage after divorce, the marriage of couples where children from earlier relationships are included, weddings where the bride does not wish to be "given away" by her father or to take her new husband's name – all kinds of different situations can be accommodated. Quite often the couple choose a very traditional ceremony, merely omitting the religious elements they would feel to be hypocritical.'

Humanist ceremonies can be conducted in almost any location. It is even possible to hold them in a private chapel – if you have access to one – or a Unitarian church, providing the minister is willing to give permission. If the chapel or church is registered for the solemnization of marriage, the ceremony will be legally binding providing the set form of words required by law (see above) is included.

The Humanist Association will provide a list of celebrants in your area and you are free to choose the person you feel most comfortable with. You can also ask a family friend or relative to conduct the ceremony for you if you wish. The content of the ceremony and the form it will take are decided by the couple in discussion with the celebrant. The basic focus of the marriage is the love, commitment and respect offered by one partner to the other, as well as responsibility for the children of the relationship. Humanists affirm sexual equality in the context of a wider concern for humanity, and the content of the ceremony will reflect this. The ceremonies usually include a number of readings of both poetry and prose chosen by the couple.

A Humanist ceremony might take the following form:

- Opening words of welcome, which may include a statement or explanation of Humanist values in marriage.
- Thoughts on marriage. This might include readings either by the celebrant, family or friends, or by the couple themselves.
- Declarations of commitment, or vows. Couples can write their own, or use promises adapted from other traditions.
- Use of symbols, e.g. the exchange of rings or other tokens; the lighting of candles; drinking from the same cup (as in the Jewish tradition).
- Expressions of support for the couple from family and friends.
- Closing words and an expression of hopes for the future.

The ceremony can be constructed to involve children of the family, or to take account of previous relationships. Absent friends or relatives can also be included – in one ceremony mention was made of the bride's much loved grandmother who had died the previous month. Further information, as well as lists of accredited Humanist celebrants can be found on **www.humanism.org.uk/ weddings.asp**.

PAGAN

There are several forms of pagan ceremony which can be adapted, from a simple 'New Age' handfasting to a formal Druid wedding rite. Locations such as Glastonbury Tor and other ancient sites on common land may be used for such ceremonies, but permission must be obtained to hold ceremonies at monuments on English Heritage or National Trust sites. This is unlikely to be given for somewhere like Stonehenge, but Castlerigg Stone Circle, set in the Lake District mountains and owned by the National Trust, has already been used for such a ceremony. Stone circles which have open access, such as Avebury in Wiltshire and Long Meg near Penrith in Cumbria – both of which have roads running through them – are very easy to use. Scotland has many fine ancient sites, even if some of them are a little remote.

Pagans vow to honour 'both male and female aspects of the divine reality'. They believe in the unity of humankind with nature – peace, love for all things and the sanctity of life, green growing, swimming or flying, on four legs or two, are paramount. A typical pagan is one 'whose soul has been deeply touched by Nature, someone for whom the stars speak their graceful silent poetry, for whom the grasses and the deep woods are as cathedrals of the soul'. These beliefs are reflected in their rites.

A NEW AGE HANDFASTING

'Handfasting' is an old Anglo-Saxon term for an agreement between two people who wanted to be married. It was a simple ritual performed 'in the sight of the gods', though not necessarily religious – like the basis of our Christian ceremonies, its roots were in private contract. Shaking hands on a contract is still done today and most wedding ceremonies involve the couple taking each other by the hand. Roman wedding rings showed two left hands clasped together as a symbol of their union. A handfasting traditionally lasted for a year and a day and was then renewed – or not, as the couple decided! Modern pagans celebrate handfastings for life, as well as a special ceremony where couples may pledge themselves for eternity – the Karmic link.

Modern settings for ceremonies include fields, premises licensed for weddings such as country houses, gardens, woodland glades, stone circles or even old Celtic hillforts. Celebrants can be contacted through the Pagan Federation.

Kate and Stephen decided to have a handfasting ceremony to follow their civil marriage. They chose Annie Wildwood, a Celtic priestess from the Dragonpaths organization, as their celebrant. Annie's practice is to discuss the format with the couple beforehand to find out what they would like. Some want a formal pagan ceremony, others simply want a vaguely 'New Age' earth-centred wedding in a beautiful open-air setting. There are many options; some brides like to have a procession with flower maidens, some like to include the 'jumping the broomstick' ritual, and there are favourite readings and music they may want to have incorporated into the ceremony.

The basic ritual, which Kate and Stephen chose, is a blend of Celtic and folk tradition and involves a chalice, bread, wine and the symbols of the Four Elements – water for West, stone or crystal for North, charcoal or incense for East, candles or a candle lantern for South. Annie began by casting a circle with flower petals or grains, to symbolize the encircling horizon and the meeting point of Sky and Earth. It is a sacred space, representing the cyclical nature of life: rebirth, childhood, maturity and death. It is also a symbol of the care and protection offered by the home. Altars were placed at the four cardinal points. The chalice and the rings that the couple were going to exchange were placed on the altar of the North – the direction which symbolizes love and passion. The other symbols were placed on their appropriate altars.

The couple stood in the centre of the circle with Annie, who in her role as priestess invoked the powers of the Four Directions, the Earth, the Sky and the spirits of the land. Then friends of both Kate and Stephen read favourite poems and a Celtic blessing. A folk singer friend of Kate's sang an unaccompanied Gaelic air.

Then, taking bread from the altar, Annie offered a piece to each participant, saying as she did so, 'May the fruitfulness of Earth be with you.' Then she offered the chalice of wine, saying, 'May the love of Spirit be with you.'

Kate and Stephen exchanged their rings and made the vows of commitment to each other that they had previously written, with Annie's guidance. Annie then declared that they were both, by their own free will, united in marriage and she gave them formally into each other's hands. They then left the circle by leaping over the broomstick – a symbol to represent stepping over the threshold of their new life together.

Other couples who have been married in this way, some of whom chose to have a register office ceremony as well (in order for the union to be legally recognized), have been delighted with the result. Comments such as 'I've never been to a wedding wearing wellies!' from the bride's grandmother after tramping through a field of cows, or the bride and groom's ecstatic 'It was so beautiful when that robin began singing – I'll never forget this day!' are typical. One couple who chose a pagan handfasting in a spectacular stone circle in the Lake District told me that it was the most moving event in their lives – the setting as awe-inspiring as a cathedral. 'It was magical. We really felt we were under the eyes of the gods.'

DRUID WEDDING CEREMONY

The celebrants are a Druid and a Druidess. Guests form a horseshoe and the participants then form a circle within it, cast by the Druid and consecrated by the Druidess. The circle is divided by four Gates on the four points of the compass.

The celebrants welcome everyone to the ceremony and invoke the blessing of the Four Directions. Then the Druid declares: *We stand upon this holy earth and in the face of heaven to witness the sacred rite of marriage between [name] and [name]. Just as we come together as family and friends so we ask for the Greater Powers to be present here within our Circle. May this sacred union be filled with their holy presence.*

The power of the God and Goddess are also invoked. The Druidess then says: *The joining together of man and woman in the sacred Rite of Marriage brings together great forces from which may flow the seeds of future generations to be nurtured within the womb of time. Within every masculine nature lies the feminine; within every feminine nature lies the masculine. The interplay of masculine and feminine forces when flowing freely in a union based upon true love finds many expressions. This union is truly holy.*

Druid: *Goddess to God.*
1st Woman: *God to Goddess.*
lst Man: *Priestess to Priest.*

2nd Woman: *Priest to Priestess.*
2nd Man: *Woman to Man.*
3rd Woman: *Man to Woman.*
3rd Man: *Mother to Son.*
4th Woman: *Son to Mother.*
4th Man: *Daughter to Father.*
5th Woman: *Father to Daughter.*
5th Man: *Sister to Brother.*
Druidess: *Brother to Sister.*
Druid: *Who walks the path of the moon to stand before heaven and declare her sacred vows?*

[The woman to be married steps forward]

Druid: *Do you [name] come to this place of your own free will?*
Woman: *I do.*
Druidess: *Who walks the path of the sun to stand upon this holy earth and declare his sacred vows?*

[The man to be married steps forward]

Druidess: *Do you [name] come to this place of your own free will?*
Man: *I do.*

[Both must walk the symbolic paths of the sun and moon, clockwise and anti-clockwise, around the circle returning to the eastern Gate]

Druid: *[Name] and [name], you have walked the circles of the sun and moon, will you now walk together the circle of Time, travelling through the Elements and the Seasons?*
Couple: *We will.*

[Both walk, holding hands, to the southern Gate]

South: *Will your love survive the harsh fires of change?*
Couple: *It will.*
South: *Then accept the blessing of the Element of Fire in this, the place of Summer. May your home be filled with warmth.*

[Both walk to the western Gate]

West: *Will your love survive the ebb and flow of feeling?*
Couple: *It will.*
West: *Then accept the blessing of the Element of Water in this, the place of Autumn. May your life together be filled with love.*

[Both walk to the northern Gate]

North: *Will your love survive the times of stillness and restriction?*
Couple: *It will.*
North: *Then accept the blessing of the Element of Earth in this, the place of Winter. May your union be strong and fruitful.*

[Both walk to the eastern Gate]

East: *Will your love survive the clear light of day?*
Couple: *It will.*
East: *Then accept the blessing of the Element of Air in this, the place of Spring. May your marriage be blessed by the light of every new dawn.*
Druidess: *All things in Nature are circular – night becomes day, day becomes night and night becomes day again. The moon waxes and wanes and waxes again. There is Spring, Summer, Autumn, Winter and then the Spring returns. These things are part of the Great Mysteries.*
[Name] and [Name], do you bring your symbols of these Great Mysteries of Life?
Couple: *We do.*
Druid: *Then, before all present, repeat these words.*
Woman [Facing the man in order to give him a ring]: *Accept in freedom this circle of gold as a token of my vows. With it I pledge my love, my strength and my friendship. I bring you joy now and for ever. I vow upon this holy earth that through you I will honour all men.*
Man [Facing the woman and giving her a ring]: *Accept in freedom this circle of gold as a token of my vows. With it I pledge my love, my strength and my friendship. I bring you joy now and for ever. I vow in the face of heaven that through you I will honour all women.*
Woman: *In the name of the Goddess I bring you the warmth of my heart.* [She is handed a lighted taper by her First Woman (mother or friend)]
Man: *In the name of the God of love I bring you the light of my love.* [He is handed a lighted taper by his First Man (father or friend)]

[Both then light a single candle in the centre]

> All: *May the warmth and the light of your union be blessed.*
> Druid: *Do you swear upon the sword of justice to keep sacred your vows?*
> Couple: *We swear.*
> Druidess: *Then seal your promise with a kiss.*
> Druid: *Beneficent spirits and the souls of our ancestors, accept the union of your children. Help them, guide them, protect and bless their home and the children born of their union. May their life together reflect the harmony of all life in its perfect union. May they work together in times of ease and times of hardship, knowing that they are truly blessed. From this time forth you walk together along Life's Path: may your way be blessed.*

[Both walk together clockwise around the circle to be greeted by the participants, finishing at the western Gate.]

After the celebrants thank the Four Directions, the participants are instructed to make the three circles of existence. The couple hold hands to make a circle within the circle. Participants in the horseshoe join hands to form a third.

> All: *We swear by peace and love to stand*
> *Heart to heart and hand in hand*
> *Mark O Spirit and hear us now*
> *Confirming this our Sacred Vow.*

Druid: *This sacred Rite of Marriage ends in peace, as in peace it began. Let us withdraw, holding peace and love in our hearts until we meet again.*

The full ceremony is given in Philip Carr-Gomm's book *The Druid Way*.

JEWISH

Like the Quakers, Jewish synagogues can register their own marriages which can take place on any day of the week except religious festivals and the Sabbath (Saturday). Tuesday is regarded as a particularly auspicious day. Jews are exempt from the usual restrictions of time and place, so weddings can be celebrated out of doors and at any time of the day – traditionally in the afternoon or early evening, so that the couple have time to reflect on the commitment they are about to make. Devout Jews may spend the day in prayer and sometimes forgo food before the ceremony. An Orthodox bride will also go to the mikveh, a ritual bath, a few days before the ceremony.

Jewish brides are married under a canopy, the chuppah. In poorer countries this is sometimes just a prayer shawl, or embroidered cloth held over the heads of the bride and groom, but more usually it is a ceremonial canopy with four wooden poles decorated for the occasion by flowers. The canopy is supposed to represent harmony, and the home that the couple will create together. The marriage ceremony is performed by a rabbi in the presence of a quorum of ten Jewish men.

On entering the synagogue, the bride's veil is lifted back to reveal her face. The groom comes to greet her with his attendants, some carrying candles, and places the veil over her face. This custom originated in the story of Jacob, who was tricked into marrying Leah instead of Rachel, because he could not see who was under the veil.

The groom is led by the bride's father to the chuppah while the choir sing, *'He who is mighty, Blessed and Great above all things, may he bless the Bride and Bridegroom.'* The bride follows, accompanied by her mother and mother-in-law, carrying candles, and stands next to the groom. In some ceremonies the bride is led around the groom seven times. The first blessing is sung over wine in a silver cup for 'there is no joyous celebration without wine' and both bride and groom sip from the cup. Then the betrothal is blessed with a prayer of praise and thanksgiving and the groom places the ring on the bride's finger saying, *'Behold you are consecrated to me with this ring in accordance with the Law of Moses and Israel.'* If the ceremony is being conducted in a Reform synagogue, the bride will give the groom a ring and make the same declaration. The marriage contract or *Ketubah* – a form of pre-nuptial agreement – is read by the presiding rabbi and the Seven Benedictions are recited either by him, or by the guests. The groom crushes a glass symbolically under his foot and then the guests shout *'Mazel tov'* – good luck! – to the couple.

The wording and format of the Jewish marriage contract are of great antiquity. Written in Aramaic, it is 'a legally binding document of confidence and trust which lists the husband's obligations to his wife', including his duty to feed, clothe and care for her, under Jewish law. They are often drawn up by an artist.

Jewish weddings are joyful affairs which include music and dancing and celebrate marriage as 'a gift bestowing joy and blessing, goodness, security and peace'. The festivities continue for seven days, when the couple open the doors of their new home to receive visitors, and friends and family throw parties for them in the evening.

Orthodox Jews do not usually allow intermarriage. Reform and Progressive Jews do. The non-Jewish partner is generally expected to convert to Judaism, but even if they do not, it is sometimes possible to find a rabbi prepared to conduct the ceremony. In Great Britain and America, the incidence of intermarriage in the years 1985–90 had risen to 57 per cent of all Jews getting married and figures informally available for 1990–95 show an even higher proportion.

Marriage customs of the couple's host country can be incorporated into the Jewish ceremony, providing they don't have their origins in another religion. So bridesmaids and a best man are permitted and the bride can wear the traditional white dress and veil of European marriage. The bride and groom's attendants can be non-Jews, since they are not part of the religious significance of the ceremony.

An illuminated Jewish marriage contract (or *Ketubah*).
By Juliet Levy ©

BUDDHIST

There are almost as many different forms of Buddhist teaching as there are Christian denominations. Buddhists generally try to follow the Ten Precepts, which are very similar to the Ten Commandments and outline the rules by which a Buddhist should live. These involve vows of non-violence, chastity, truth, temperance, self-control and respect for others.

Marriage has no religious significance to a Buddhist and so there is no set Buddhist marriage ceremony. In other countries (such as India, China and Japan), Buddhist couples are married according to the local cultural customs. In China, the bride was usually collected from her home in a decorated chair or carriage, by the groom's family. She would be dressed in a red robe, with a red veil over her face. Her parents went through a ritual grieving rite. Then the bride was carried through the streets to the groom's house. There, two red candles and three sticks of incense would be lit before the gods of Heaven and Earth and the bride and groom would pay homage to the household gods and their ancestors.

British Buddhists usually have a simple civil ceremony. Since this does not allow any religious content to be included, there can be no readings from Buddhist texts, mantras and prayers. If the couple want to have a ritual blessing, it would have to be performed at a separate ceremony. If you are being married in a hotel, or other licensed building – anywhere other than a register office

– this could follow immediately after the civil one, provided that the registrar has left the premises, or you have moved into another room.

A Buddhist marriage might include an exchange of white silk scarves – symbols of spiritual light and love – and the 'ceremony of the cups', which is practised in Japan. A cup, or glass, of saki is offered to the bride and groom three times and each time they take three sips from it as a symbol of sharing and unity.

HINDU

The Hindu religion is believed to be the most ancient in the world. Its sacred texts include the Rig-Veda, the Upanishads, the Mahabharata and the Bhagavadgita. It is a coalition of a number of beliefs with a bewildering number of different gods and has been described as 'more a culture than a creed'. Originating in the Indus valley, its teachings have spread across Europe, where the establishment of ashrams, the practice of transcendental meditation, and the influence of teachers such as Ramakrishna have been growing since the nineteenth century when Madame Blavatsky popularized their message. This culminated in a huge surge of interest in the 1960s and 1970s when high-profile figures like John Lennon and Paul McCartney stayed in ashrams and inspired a cult following for the Maharishi Mahesh Yogi. Hindu beliefs have been absorbed into Western culture to an astonishing degree. Many of us use the word 'karma', practise yoga, embrace vegetarianism and mutual toleration and respect the world influence of Mahatma Ghandi without really knowing what Hinduism is.

Most Hindu marriages are arranged by the families, sometimes when the children are quite young. This practice is now being discouraged and the Indian government has introduced age limits for legal marriage – eighteen for girls and twenty-one for boys. When a marriage is discussed between the families, the boy will be brought to the girl's house by his father and the couple will be left alone to talk while their fathers discuss terms. Both the boy and the girl will then be asked whether they are willing to consent to the marriage.

At the engagement ceremony eleven men, prominent in the community, but not related to the couple, must be present as witnesses to what is a formal agreement involving the transfer of the dowry – which can be substantial. The groom's family often give jewellery. The payment of dowries has become such a problem for families who are not wealthy that the Indian government has tried to put an end to it, though the tradition is very strong.

A few days before the marriage the bride is washed with sandalwood paste and turmeric powder. This removes body hair and gives the skin a golden glow. The day before the ceremony her hands are painted with henna in intricate designs. After that both bride and groom are supposed to remain at home until the marriage.

As marriage is a family occasion, it is traditional for

the ceremonies to take place in the bride's home and not in a temple. But, as most houses are too small for the large numbers of invited guests and extended family, most marriages are now celebrated at a Marriage Hall, which becomes the bride's house for the day. In some parts of India weddings take place very early in the morning; others, such as Punjabi ceremonies, are celebrated in the afternoon. The bride is brought to the Hall by her mother's brother, accompanied by her family. The groom arrives later with his family, brought by his sister's husband. The bride traditionally wears a sari lavishly embroidered in gold thread, bought for her by the groom's family. In some areas of India the sari will be red, although green is sometimes worn. There are two priests, one for the bride and the other for the groom, and there is a ceremonial fire in the room. The couple stand in the middle of the room, facing each other, separated by a curtain held up between them. Verses are recited by the priests from holy texts and the couple are declared to be married. The curtain is removed and the musicians begin to play. The bride takes the floral garland from her own neck and places it around her husband's, and he does the same for her. They are showered with rice and flower petals and blessed by the guests while trays of sweets are distributed.

After the wedding there are a number of smaller traditional ceremonies. The groom places the sindoor on his wife's forehead – the circle of red powder that indicates that she is now a married woman. He gives the bride her new name and her mother-in-law has to call her by it three times. Her new name will also be written in rice. The bride and groom both wear shawls for their wedding and these are untied afterwards by the bride's sister. Popped rice (similar to popped corn) is thrown into the fire by the bride's brother. The bride and groom are then walked around the ceremonial fire seven times. The groom also gives his wife the mangal sudra – a necklace worn by married women.

Vashti, a Brahmin brought up and educated in England, met her English husband when she went back to India for her sister's wedding. David was working for one of the aid agencies. They wrote to each other when Vashti came back to Birmingham; after David's overseas contract expired they saw each other frequently and soon decided that they wanted to marry. Vashti accepted that it would be difficult to have a traditional Hindu wedding and together she and David created a special ceremony to be held in a local hotel. The registrar was booked to conduct a civil marriage and then Vashti and David moved into the reception room for the rest of the proceedings so as not to infringe the law on civil marriages. Vashti was dressed in a beautiful red and gold sari and a local florist had created floral garlands for her and David. Verses were read from Hindu scriptures and the hotel provided a portable charcoal brazier for the fire so that all the small ceremonies could be carried out. Guests threw rice, and rose petals. Indian musicians played during the lavish meal that followed and they also accompanied an Indian Kathak dancer who was happy to explain the significance of the various intricate dance patterns to English guests unfamiliar with the art form. Vashti's father joked about his relief at not having to pay a large sum of money to persuade David to marry his daughter and everyone agreed that it was one of the best weddings they'd ever been to.

MUSLIM

Marriage is of great importance in Islam, since Muslims believe that Allah created 'men and women as companions for one another, so that they can procreate and live in peace and tranquillity according to the commandments of Allah and the directions of His Messenger'. The regulation of marriage is contained in the Shariah, the Islamic code of law.

Men and women are entitled to see each other before marriage to make sure that they are not repugnant to each other, though in some countries this 'viewing' can be quite perfunctory. The Koran also insists on the consent of both parties to the marriage, though in practice a woman's choice (but not a man's) may be overruled by her father. If a man or a woman is forced to marry someone they do not like, it is grounds for divorce. Marriage is a solemn contract between the man and the woman. Remarriage of widows and divorcees is allowed, but in the stricter sects is subject to the same parental overview.

There is a comprehensive list of the degrees of relationship that prohibit marriage. These include a step-parent (however briefly s/he may have been married to a parent), stepbrothers and sisters, foster brothers and sisters, foster parents and their close relatives, and stepchildren, as well as the usual list of close blood relatives. A man is allowed to have up to four wives at any one time.

The basic Muslim marriage ceremony consists of three parts, the Henna Nights (usually two), the wedding ceremony itself and the family celebration, which does not take place on the day, but only after the bride has spent her first night with the bridegroom and paid her ritual visit as a married woman to her parents' home. The wedding feast is often held in a hotel, days, sometimes weeks, later, and can be a very lavish affair. When Noor (an Asian Muslim) married Paul (an English Christian who converted to Islam so as not to alienate Noor's family) they had an adapted ceremony that was less elaborate than it would have been had they both come from Muslim families, and Noor also had an English civil ceremony in a hotel.

The henna ceremonies take place on the nights before the wedding. The bride and her female friends and family will take henna and perfumed oil to the groom's house, where the henna is ritually placed in his hands (often on a tissue so that the hands are not stained) and he is anointed with the oil. There is a celebration with singing and dancing. On the second night, the groom and his family bring henna and oil to the bride's house. Ceremonial money is also given, but this is usually donated to charity. It is traditional for the bride to wear yellow for this and to be 'dressed down' for the occasion so that she will look more sumptuous on her wedding day. Her hands are painted with intricate designs in henna. Noor's English bridesmaids also had their hands hennaed for the occasion.

The wedding ceremony doesn't take place in a mosque, and can be held in the bride's own home, or in a hotel or hired hall. The bride and groom arrive separately – the groom accompanied by his own father and the bride's, and other male relatives who will act as witnesses. The bride arrives with both mothers and her female attendants. It is traditional for the bride, her attendants and her family to be dressed in specially embroidered, elaborate costumes. The bride may wear the lankah, a short tunic over a heavily embroidered skirt or pantaloons, and a shawl. The couple sit in different rooms. The mullah who officiates goes first to the bride and asks her if she agrees to the marriage. This is a very important part of the proceedings and if she does not give her consent the marriage will not take place. Sometimes the mullah will ask the bride to repeat a section from the Koran.

The mullah then goes back into the main room where the groom and the witnesses are sitting and asks the groom to repeat certain passages from the Koran. All the witnesses present must cover their heads out of respect. Prayers are said for the couple and the mullah will then ask the groom if he agrees to the amount of the dowry offered by the bride's father, which he must formally accept. This money, a nominal £50 in Noor's case, is supposed to be money held in trust by the groom for his wife if the marriage breaks down. Once the money has been handed over, blessings are said by the mullah and the bride is brought in to join her husband. In some ceremonies they sit together on a raised dais so that everyone can see them, and some couples drink from the same cup to symbolize their union.

Noor and Paul chose to combine the wedding feast with their English civil marriage in a hotel a week later and Noor wore a traditional white wedding dress for the occasion.

SAME-SEX UNIONS

Both male and female homosexuals form long-term, lasting relationships and want them recognized. Greenland, Iceland, Denmark, Norway and Sweden have partnership laws and it is possible to be married in a civil ceremony. Similarly, marriage – or 'registration of partnership' with the same civil rights as a married heterosexual couple – has just been made legal in Holland. Certain American states, like California, also offer a 'Declaration of Domestic Partnership' for same-sex relationships. There is even a church – the Metropolitan Community Church of Los Angeles – where same-sex unions can be celebrated. In Britain, marriage between people of the same sex is not legally recognized, though a cohabitation agreement would have the same legal effect as any other kind of contract and there are a number of organizations which will offer ceremonies of blessing on such a relationship.

Originating in America in 1968, the Universal Fellowship of Metropolitan Community Churches has more than three hundred churches worldwide. In Britain it has branches in London, Bournemouth and Manchester (see Useful Addresses). They are pledged to meet the spiritual needs of the gay and lesbian community and are dedicated to emotional healing and reconciliation. They conduct ceremonies of union and blessing for gays, lesbians and transsexuals. Their celebrants are also willing to travel to conduct ceremonies in other places.

Ceremonies which celebrate the union of man with man and woman with woman have a long history, dating back to the Greeks and Romans. John Boswell, a Yale historian, has researched the subject extensively; his book *The Marriage of Likeness* details many recorded relationships accepted and celebrated by the early Christian church, including Saints Serge and Bacchus and the early female martyrs Perpetua and Felicitas. Not only were same-sex unions accepted, there is a body of church liturgy for the celebration of such unions and several examples appear in translation as an appendix to the book.

The extract below comes from Belgrade and was part of a Slavonic (pre-eighteenth-century) Order for the Celebration of the Union of Two Men but it could very easily be adapted for the union of two women, perhaps by inserting the names of Naomi and Ruth, Felicitas and Perpetua in place of the paired male saints.

The priest places the right hands of both men upon the Bible. In some ceremonies a candle or a cross is placed in their left hands. The priest then recites an invocation, followed by the Lord's Prayer, and this is followed by a hymn or anthem.

Then the priest takes his scarf – 'the holy belt' – and ties it around the two who hold it with their left hands.

Let us pray. Oh Lord, Our God, who hast vouchsafed unto us the promise of salvation, and hast commanded us to love one another and to forgive one another our trespasses, Thou art the Author of grace and Friend of mankind, accept Thou these thy two servants [name] and [name], who love each other with a love of the spirit, and have desired to come into thy holy church, and grant unto them hope, unashamed faithfulness and true love. As Thou didst bestow upon Thy holy disciples and apostles peace and love, grant these also the same, O Christ our Lord, and vouchsafe unto them every promise of salvation and life everlasting. For to Thee do we give glory.

Second Prayer: *Lord God almighty, who didst fashion human kind after thine image and likeness and bestow upon us eternal life, Thou thoughtest it right that thy holy and glorious apostles Peter and Paul, and Philip and Bartholomew, should be joined together in perfect love, faith and love of the heart. Thou also didst deem it proper for the holy martyrs Serge and Bacchus to be united. Bless Thou these thy servants, grant unto them grace and prosperity, and faith and love; let them love each other without envy and without temptation all the days of their lives, through the power of the Holy Spirit and the prayers of our Holy Queen, the Mother of God*

65

and ever-virgin Mary, and all thy saints, who worship Thee through the ages. For Thine is the power and thine the kingdom, Father, Son and Holy Spirit, now and for ever and ever.

There follow blessings and readings from the New Testament, in particular the first epistle of Paul to the Corinthians, chapter 13, verses 1–8, 'Though I speak with the tongues of men and of angels . . .', and Psalm 133, 'Behold, how good and how pleasant it is for brethren to dwell together in unity!' Extracts from the Song of Songs would also be appropriate.

The Unitarian Church has a liberal attitude to same-sex unions, although the views of individual ministers may differ. Some ministers are willing to conduct ceremonies for both gay and lesbian couples. There is now also a strong Lesbian and Gay Christian Movement and it is possible to arrange for sympathetic clergy among their members to conduct a service of blessing for a same-sex relationship. There is similar support for same-sex couples among the Jewish community.

Many neo-pagan/Celtic celebrants will perform a handfasting ceremony, the content and format of which can be decided by discussion with both partners. Becky Butler, in her anthology of female same-sex unions, *Ceremonies of the Heart*, records the experience of Noreen and Helen, both feminist pagans from New Zealand, who decided to have a commitment ceremony on the beach below Noreen's beach house and adapted a ceremony from Zsuzsanna Budapest's *Holy Book of Women's Mysteries*.

A circle was drawn up on the beach with tamarisk branches and they constructed an altar with two pottery chalices, a tray of fruit, nuts and vegetables, and bowls of white and yellow flowers. They also had a branch of myrtle, the symbolic tree of love, for the broomstick. There were thirteen women, the traditional number for a pagan coven, and the ceremony was led by three close friends.

For those without religious beliefs, some Humanist celebrants are prepared to conduct same-sex marriages, otherwise a simple commitment ceremony (see overleaf) might be appropriate. Most lesbian and gay couples write their own scripts, since there are so few established rites of passage for same-sex unions. It can be a very creative experience. As one gay couple said, 'Writing your own material causes you to think very deeply about your relationship and about your reasons for wanting a ceremony in the first place.' Many couples, brought up within established cultures, prefer to adapt a traditional ceremony rather than create something new.

Rebecca and Tess, two social workers in their thirties, wanted to have a commitment ceremony that would reflect their diverse religious backgrounds. Rebecca's parents are non-practising Jews and Tess was brought up as a Roman Catholic. Their ceremony took place in the garden under a specially designed canopy. Blessings, carefully rewritten to reflect the feminine rather than the masculine, were recited in both Hebrew and English, with wine and candles, by a sympathetic female rabbi. They wrote their own vows, using the Christian marriage service as a guide – 'The words are so beautiful we couldn't improve on them' – and friends read poetry from Kahlil Gibran and the Song of Solomon. The traditional glass was crushed underfoot at the close of the ceremony. They had traditional Jewish music and had asked a friend to draw up a special ketubah – the Jewish marriage contract – for the occasion.

Other Jewish same-sex couples have adapted the Jewish wedding ceremony to fit their circumstances and coined the phrase Brit Ahavah – literally 'covenant of love' – to describe their ceremony. In creating such a ceremony there is tremendous scope for innovation. One couple had a banner inscribed with the Hebrew words 'Tikkun Olam' which means 'the healing of the world'. Another couple had their rings engraved with the traditional inscription 'Ahoovot Chaiim' – Beloveds for Life. Both these couples were lucky, in that they were able to have a synagogue ceremony at the Congregation Beth Simchat Torah, the gay and lesbian synagogue in New York.

A SIMPLE CEREMONY OF COMMITMENT

The couple should face each other and hold each other's hands. Then each person should repeat the following words, spoken together if they wish to do so.

I declare in front of all the people we have invited here today, that out of all the men/women I have known, I have chosen you to walk with me to the end of the road, wherever that might be.

The sharing of a small piece of bread and a glass of wine:

I share this bread and wine with you as a public demonstration of my promise to share whatever I have with you, be it little or much.

The exchange of rings (these can be of woven textile or the plaited stems of plant or leaf rather than the traditional gold or silver), earrings or other jewellery:

I give you this ring as a token of my love for you and as a symbol of my commitment. As this ring freely encircles your finger, I promise that the windows and doors of the house that we shall build together shall always be open.

I promise to love, respect and trust you. Your dreams shall be my dreams, your joy, my joy. When you are ill, I will be beside you. When you need me, I will support you. When we are apart, I will be with you in spirit. I wish never to be a burden or a hindrance in our life together, but a helpmate, a companion and a friend. I do not expect it always to be easy, but promise to do my best even through the difficult times, in order to build something of value.

I ask all these people here today to help and support me to honour the promises I have made.

Creating Your Own Ceremony

Be very clear about the kind of ceremony you want to have. Large, or small and intimate? Formal or informal? Don't be put off by the reactions of relatives to the idea of an unusual form of ceremony. If you do it well, they will all enjoy it.

Where are you going to hold the wedding? Unusual venues, such as stone circles, beaches, underwater, will require a certain amount of organization to transport invited guests.

Do you want a religious element, or is it to be strictly secular? Do you want simply to adapt and extend the standard civil ceremony, or to have a separate one of your own afterwards? Bear in mind that you will have to wait until the registrar has left the premises, or move into another room, if you want to include any religious (or even simply vaguely spiritual) material.

Do you want a processional ceremony, perhaps with candles, flowers, music and attendants? Are you going to use traditional symbols: rings, candles, salt, wine and bread, flowers and canopies?

It's important that guests know in advance what type of event they're coming to, so that they are suitably dressed. High heels and a large hat are not exactly practical for a muddy walk to a woodland glade, or staggering down a cliff path! It is no longer necessary to observe the strict form of words that used to make wedding invitations so stiff and formal. Many couples dislike the idea that the bride's family alone should have the right to invite the guests. Informal variations such as 'The Jones family and the Smith family invite you to the wedding of Sarah and Peter', or 'Sarah Jones and Peter Smith invite you to help them celebrate their wedding' are perfectly acceptable. Where there are children, the wording could be as follows: 'Melanie and Lucy Jones and David Smith invite you to the wedding of their parents Sarah and Peter'.

Provide an order of service so that the guests can follow the ceremony. This is particularly important if you are having something unusual. People like to feel that they are part of things. Computer design packages and laser photocopiers have made designing and printing your own invitations and programmes very easy. Commercial printing has come down in price accordingly.

Flowers are a very important part of a wedding ceremony. If you're having a church or chapel wedding, your floral decorations will have to fit in with the church calendar and any other wedding that is taking place on that day. For a register office ceremony it is often impossible to have your own flower arrangements. This should be discussed with the registrar when you book. Hotels and other venues are more flexible. It can sometimes be difficult to find unconventional floral arrangements. If the florists in your area only offer a limited catalogue of set pieces, the market gardeners or wholesalers will occasionally supply direct and may know someone who is willing to do unusual displays. There are often local guilds of flower arrangers some of whom may be skilled in the art of floral decoration.

If you don't like the idea of so many flowers being 'wasted' for the day, think about using arrangements of plants and shrubs. These can sometimes be hired from firms that specialize in supplying plants for offices, hotel foyers and conferences. Bay trees in pairs, decorated with ribbon, would look very good on either side of a processional route. Roses or white lilies can be planted in big pots for a vivid floral display. Rosemary, lavender and jasmine fill the room with scent.

Apart from decorating every available space in the venue with plants and flowers, there are other ways in which flowers can be employed. The bride and groom could be married under a floral arch or a canopy decorated with flowers. Small children can be given baskets of dried flower petals to scatter on the ground in front of the bridal pair. In medieval times, strewing herbs (strongly scented herbs such as camomile, rosemary, thyme or rue) were scattered for the bride to walk on. Floral crowns and garlands are traditional in other cultures and are very pretty. In some parts of Europe, the bride's bouquet is arranged around a candle placed inside a glass and this is lit just before she walks up the aisle. Elizabethan posies of mixed flowers and herbs, or the informal, trailing bouquets of flowers and evergreen material that were fashionable in Edwardian times make very attractive alternatives to the stiff and heavily wired formal bouquet offered by many florists. In previous centuries, brides have sometimes carried baskets of flowers tied with ribbon. This is quite practical, since the basket can be filled with water-retentive material and the flowers will last a long time. One bride recently carried a basket of dried flowers, herbs and leaves which she now keeps on her dressing table. She could also have filled the basket with flowering plants for the day.

Are you going to provide buttonholes and corsages for the guests? You could adopt a custom from Europe where children of the family stand in the doorway with baskets of flowers and give one to each guest. These are then thrown at the bride and groom after the marriage rather like confetti!

Do you want a formal meal, a banquet, a buffet, a barbeque or a picnic? If you're having an unusual themed wedding the food can be designed to match – anything from a medieval feast or Roman orgy to a formal Regency dinner. There are a number of excellent books on the history of food if you want to plan something different. It's also fun to incorporate customs from other countries. In China they use wonderful ice sculptures – swans, pagodas, trees – as the centrepiece for the table; in France the wedding cake is a tower of profiteroles drizzled with chocolate; elsewhere in Europe guests are served with trays of sugared almonds, Turkish delight and marzipan sweetmeats while they wait. Whatever it is, make sure the guests know what to expect. The timing of the ceremony can sometimes mean that there is a long, hungry gap between the marriage and the meal. I have vivid memories of travelling some distance to arrive at the church half an hour before a one o'clock wedding, with no time for lunch. After photographs and the transfer to the hotel, a long reception line and a generous bar serving aperitifs, we eventually sat down to the meal at six o'clock almost too tired and inebriated to eat anything! Make sure, too, that people with special dietary requirements are given an option. Buddhists, Hindus, Muslims, Jews, vegetarians and vegans should be catered for. If only non-alcoholic drinks are to be served, you should also warn people in advance.

Etiquette used to demand that the bride and groom and their parents stand at the door of the reception room to welcome the guests. This can be very time-consuming and is no longer necessary if you want to have an informal ceremony. In some other cultures the bride and groom are the last at the reception and are welcomed by the guests with applause, music and the throwing of flower petals, confetti and rice. Bear in mind that guests will want to congratulate the bride and groom personally so provide space and time for the couple to talk to people during the reception.

It's becoming more common for guests to bring the present with them to the reception, rather than sending it in advance. Provide a table for gifts and allow time to open them and thank people. Keep a list – or arrange for someone else to do so – as it is all too easy to forget who gave what.

As a record of the day, it's a good idea to have a Marriage Book to be signed by the couple, the celebrant and then by all the guests who witnessed the ceremony – many of whom will want to write personal messages and good wishes. If you're not the type of person who wants a separate photograph album labelled 'Our Wedding' in gold letters, then you could add photographs in order to have a complete record.

Are you going to have a professional photographer, a video, or rely on family 'happy snaps' taken by a friend? In the past it was quite usual not to have formal photographs on the day itself (they can take a great deal of time), and couples went into a studio to have a photograph of the wedding group taken separately.

You will need to decide on the timing of the music for the ceremony, and if you are using a CD or tape player rather than live music, have someone to switch it on and off. If you're having an organist, or musicians, make sure they have the appropriate level of skill to play any complicated pieces you have chosen. If you are having a church wedding you may also want to have the bells rung. There are some suggestions for suitable music on pp. 95–100.

If you are going to have a themed wedding involving costumes, it might be easier to arrange for costume hire from a professional theatrical costumier, rather than have the guests provide their own. There are also firms who specialize in wedding costumes (see Useful Addresses).

A rehearsal is particularly important if you are having an unusual ceremony. In some ways a wedding is very similar to a theatrical production and, if it's to go smoothly, everyone needs to know what they are doing and when! At the same time, you don't want the words to be so over-rehearsed that all the spontaneity and sincerity have been taken out of them.

MARRIAGE CUSTOMS YOU MIGHT WANT TO INCORPORATE

The candle-lighting ceremony. For this, you need a three-branched candlestick. At the beginning of the ceremony the bride and the groom each light one of the candles. After they have been declared man and wife they take a taper, both holding it with their right hands, and light the central candle as a symbol of their union.

The ceremony of the cup. This is part of many traditional ceremonies including Buddhist and Jewish marriages. Wine, or other liquid, is poured into two glasses. Bride and groom pick them up in their right hands and then wrap arms before drinking out of the glass. This is then reversed so that each drinks out of the other's glass. In a variation of it, one glass or chalice is filled with liquid and offered by the celebrant to first one and then the other. In the Jewish tradition, the glass is then crushed underfoot so that no one else can drink out of it.

The Dance of Isaiah. In Greek and Russian Orthodox ceremonies the couple are led around the church three times by the celebrant after the marriage and the guests throw flowers and rice as they pass.

Bride and groom traditionally jumped over the broomstick after the marriage to symbolize crossing the threshold of their new life together. Carrying the bride over the threshold is a relic of ancient abduction ceremonies.

A thousand cranes. This is a wedding custom from the Far East where the crane (a member of the stork family) is a symbol of good fortune and fertility. Origami cranes and paper-chain cut-outs make wonderful decorations for the ceremony.

The wish tree. This could be a tree in the garden, or a branch indoors, hung with balloons and ribbons. The guests are invited to write a wish on a piece of coloured paper and tie it to the tree.

The ancient sacred marriages of the gods symbolized the union of opposites, the coming together of the male and female parts of the psyche to form a whole.

Human marriage ceremonial also celebrates this mystical union of male and female personalities into a complete, creative unit. The circle is the symbol of eternity, so the rings exchanged represent eternal love, and vows in pagan ceremonies are exchanged in a circle. Yin and Yang are the Chinese symbols for female and male, usually depicted together within a circle. It is the ultimate symbol of the union of masculine and feminine to create a whole.

Presenting the bride with a silver key. This is a relic of an old custom whereby the bride on her marriage would be given the keys of her new house and all its storecupboards. These keys came to represent her status.

Horseshoes. The horse was once worshipped as a god and appears as a magical animal in fairy tales. Its shoes are supposed to be lucky, particularly when tacked up above the new front door. It is a relic of a time when horses' skulls were either buried underneath the floorboards or attached to the gables of the house to ward off evil spirits.

It is traditional in England for the bride to carry '**something old, something new; something borrowed, something blue, and a silver shilling in her shoe**'. These are symbols of her old and her new life, the past and the future. The colour blue is associated with the Virgin Mary, with purity and fidelity. The borrowed item should come from someone who has been happy and it will then bring good luck. The silver coin is for the couple's future prosperity.

Knotted ribbons. Knots are a symbol of the binding nature of marriage, of two people being tied together. Pagan 'handfastings' involve the symbolic tying of the man and the woman's hands together with ceremonial ribbon. In Christian ceremonies the priest winds his sash around the joined hands of the bride and groom as he pronounces them man and wife. Ornamental knots of ribbons used to be given away by the newly married couple as marriage favours to the guests.

The bride's bouquet was once a potent message spelled out in the language of flowers. Lilies, associated with the Virgin Mary, are a symbol of pure, virginal love. Pink carnations were a medieval love token given at Renaissance betrothal ceremonies. Red roses stand for lasting, passionate love – traditionally there should be a dozen of them. Evergreens symbolize immortality and so eternal love – particularly laurel, the traditional symbol of victory. Herbs were carried by the bride to protect her from evil and illness, particularly rosemary, which stands for remembrance, long-lasting love and fruitfulness.

Myrtle was included in Victorian wedding bouquets as a symbol of good luck. The chief bridesmaid was expected to take a sprig of it from the bouquet and plant it in her garden. If it rooted she would get married – if it died she was fated to become an old maid! Mimosa and orange blossom are also traditionally included in the bouquet and orange blossom was often worn as a corsage or a headdress.

The bouquet is traditionally thrown as the bride leaves

for her honeymoon. The girl who catches it is supposed to be the next to be married. Many brides now opt to have their bouquets dried and preserved. They can be kept – Victorian-fashion – under a glass dome.

Apples, like orange blossom and rosemary, are a symbol of fertility. It was a Greek marriage custom for a newly married couple to divide an apple and each eat half. Apple blossom is traditionally associated with brides.

Colours are also important in a wedding ceremony. White stands for purity and innocence, red for passionate love. Yellow is associated with intellect and royalty (many queens were married in cloth of gold). Blue, often the colour of the Virgin Mary's robes in medieval iconography, symbolizes constancy and devotion. Green is the colour of freedom, beauty, laughter and a kind heart. There are certain superstitions surrounding a black wedding dress summed up in the old rhyme 'Marry in black – wish yourself back', but this probably has its origins in the fact that in our culture black is the colour of mourning. In other cultures the opposite is true and you would certainly not want to get married in white!

Getting married under a canopy, or a floral arch. The canopy could be made from velvet, embroidered or appliquéd cloth, or white linen and lace. The poles are traditionally decorated with flowers and ribbons and it is sometimes held over the bride and groom by four close friends. In some countries, the bride and groom stand under a floral arch – made from wood or bamboo, wound round with flowers and leaves. This could be static – if you were being married in the garden – or held by friends on each side indoors. This is an old medieval idea, to represent a medieval bower. Elsewhere, the custom has been reduced to the wearing of floral crowns by the bride and groom, which are changed over during the ceremony by the celebrant at the point where the exchange of rings takes place.

Leaving the wedding ceremony under an arch of honour. This used to be a feature of military marriages where a ceremonial arch of swords was provided by the groom's regimental colleagues. Variations have been created to reflect specific interests, with tennis racquets, morris dancers, poles decorated with flowers, golf clubs, horses, even spanners and wrenches for a groom who was a mechanic!

SYMBOLS

All rites and ceremonies involve the use of symbols. Symbolism is very important for our mental health. Sometimes through ritual and the use of symbols we can break through mental or emotional barriers and achieve personal growth. At various times in human history, almost every natural object in the cosmos has had some kind of symbolic significance, from the sun and the moon, rocks, animals and trees to abstract forms such as the circle and the triangle. Groups of four seem to be important in almost every culture; in our own they are represented by the Four Elements. The first of them, Air, symbolizes clear vision, inspiration, the breath of life, and the soul. Fire is a powerful, consuming force, signifying illumination, transformation, and the emotions. Earth symbolizes solidity, practicality, security, and the body; Water, purification, movement, flow, adaptability.

In creating ceremonial, a clear glass jar can be used to contain the element of Air, or more informally a bunch of balloons. Candles can be used for Fire, or a small charcoal burner. The element of Earth can be represented by a stone, a crystal, a bowl of sand or soil. Other symbolic items frequently used in rituals are pieces of wood, flowers, fruit, spices and grains. Milk, honey, wine and water also have a part to play in both Christian and more ancient forms of ceremony, representing the fertile, nurturing forces of the earth.

In pagan mythology, the Four Elements are paralleled with the Four Directions – North, South, East and West. East, where the sun rises, is associated with birth and the element of Air, represented by the Hawk of Dawn. West, where the sun sets, is the direction of death and is represented by the Salmon of Wisdom who lives in the element of Water. Cold and wintry North is represented by the Great Bear of the night sky whose domain is Earth, and the warm South equates with the element of Fire, symbolized by the Great Stag.

The circle is a very potent symbol. It has no beginning and no end, like eternity, and was used by the ancients because of its magical properties, not only as a symbol of the cyclical nature of life, but because its encircling form denoted protection. It is still a potent force today in marriage or betrothal ceremonies, where it stands for the longed-for eternal power of love.

WRITING YOUR OWN VOWS

Here are some ideas you may like to think about, with suggestions for a basic format.

Personal vows for the Bride and Groom

This is the most personal and intimate moment of the whole ceremony. Think carefully about what you want to promise each other and the wording – remember, a lot of people are going to be listening and they will be embarrassed by anything too private, sentimental or verging on the tacky. Keep it brief, simple and dignified. Use the wording of existing ceremonies as a guideline. Some people choose to give a short history of the relationship, how they met and why they have chosen that particular person. Others decide to make a statement of their hopes and desires for this relationship and what they are willing to promise the other person in order to make it work. If this doesn't appeal, then you might like to choose a poem or a piece of poetry or prose to read aloud to each other.

You could begin with a simple statement such as: 'I

have chosen you to be my partner because . . .', adding a list of the qualities you love and admire. Follow it with your promises: 'I promise to love and be faithful to you for the rest of our lives together . . .' The vows might include promises to care for the other person through difficult times, and to be forgiving and understanding. You might also want to make some reference to the joys and responsibilities of sharing.

Tess, a social worker, chose to make this simple statement to her partner in their commitment ceremony. 'I just want to say thank you, in front of all my family and friends, for coming into my life and for loving me enough to want to share it with me. It sometimes seems like a miracle, because I didn't know that I could be so happy. You have given me more than I could ever repay, but I promise that I will always try to support you, understand you, trust you and work with you to build our future together.'

In response, Tess's partner repeated the commitment spoken by Ruth to Naomi, 'Wherever you go, I will go,' and the celebrant then blessed them both with the words of the Native American blessing 'Now you will feel no rain, for each will shelter the other' (see the Anthology of Readings).

Involving the Audience

In many ceremonies the guests are passive witnesses, and are asked to contribute only when asked, at that heart-stopping moment, 'Do you know of any impediment?' Since most of the guests are either members of the family or close friends, it has become an accepted idea that they should have a more positive role in the ceremony. At the appropriate moment, the celebrant can turn to the invited guests and ask them to pledge support and encouragement for the couple.

The celebrant should turn to the witnesses and ask: *Do you, as friends and family of [name] and [name], promise to support and encourage them in their life together?*

All: *We do.*

Second Marriages

In the event of remarriage, couples may wish to acknowledge former unions and mistakes. The following is one of a number of suggested readings for a religious ceremony:

God of Love and Understanding, we know that it is impossible for people to live together without sometimes causing pain or misunderstanding. Help us to recognize our part in this failure and to know your forgiveness and the healing of the past. In particular, we ask that your love may heal any harmful memories that [name] and [name] may bring to this day.

Lift the shadow of past failures and the weight of any unhappiness. May they know your forgiveness and the peace that comes from your presence, now and always.

For a secular ceremony, something on these lines might be more appropriate:

As imperfect human beings, we recognize that it is not always possible for promises, entered into in good faith and a belief in the lasting nature of love, to be carried out. We are all fallible and often fall short of the high standards we set ourselves. We ask everyone here present to witness that we deeply regret past failures and would like to ask forgiveness for the hurt that has sometimes been the result of these mistakes. We ask their support in carrying out the commitments we have entered into today.

Dr Johnson wrote cynically that a second marriage was the triumph of Hope over Experience. We would like to affirm our belief in the value of Hope and Experience in constructing a good relationship!

A further example that could be incorporated into either a civil ceremony or a blessing is included in a new book of resources for contemporary worship called *Human Rites* and was composed by Clare Edwards.

Celebrant: *[Name] you have been married before and your marriage ended in divorce. Have you faced with honesty your part in the breakdown of that relationship?*

Response: *I have.*

Celebrant: *Have you allowed that experience to lead you into new life – to a better understanding of yourself and of your hopes and desires for the future?*

Response: *I have.*

This should be repeated for the other partner if both have been divorced. The wording is modified if either party has been widowed.

Celebrant: *[Name] you have been married before and your marriage ended with your partner's death. Have you reflected on that relationship and faced with honesty your responsibility for both its weaknesses and its strengths?*

Response: *I have.*

Celebrant: *Have you allowed the experience of that marriage to lead you into new life – to a better understanding of yourself and of your hopes and desires for the future?*

Response: *I have.*

In both cases the celebrant will say to the couple: *Owning the past, are you [name] and you [name], each now ready to give yourself fully to the new marriage relationship which you believe God is offering you?*

Both: *I am.*

Involvement of Children

Many couples now marry after they have a child, and second marriages frequently bring together the children of previous relationships. The ceremony unites the children into a new family just as it unites their parents. In almost all situations, the children can stand with their parents in front of the celebrant and take part in the ceremony. They can hold flowers, take charge of the rings or, if they are old enough, give some of the readings.

Special prayers may be included for the children of the family, or a blessing may be read by the celebrant or, if you are having a civil wedding, you may want to choose a meditation on children and family life.

Some suggestions:

Celebrant: *We ask all here present to give their blessing, support and protection to this new family, [names]. May they be surrounded by love, security and a sense of belonging.*

or:

Parenthood does not begin with the birth of the child, nor with the germination of the seed. It has its beginnings even before the child's conception, and is part and parcel of the marriage and the love from the expression of which the baby owes his being. If this is so our abilities as good mothers and fathers – and our failures too – cannot be viewed in isolation, apart from the sum total – the interaction and fusing of personalities – which makes up the marriage.

(Sheila Kitzinger, *The Experience of Childbirth*)

or:

Your children are not your children.
They are the sons and daughters of Life's longing for
   itself.

They come through you but not from you.
And though they are with you yet they belong not to
     you.

You may give them your love but not your thoughts,
For they have their own thoughts.
You may house their bodies but not their souls,
For their souls dwell in the house of tomorrow, which
     you cannot visit, not even in your dreams.
You may strive to be like them, but seek not to make
     them like you.
For life goes not backward nor tarries with yesterday.

You are the bows from which your children as living
     arrows are sent forth.
The archer sees the mark upon the path of the infinite
     and he bends with his might that his arrows may go
     swift and far.
Let your bending in the archer's hand be for gladness;
For even as he loves the arrow that flies, so he loves
     also the bow that is stable.

Kahlil Gibran, *The Prophet*

or a Celtic blessing:

Goodness of sea be yours,
Goodness of earth be yours
Goodness of heaven.

Each day be joyous to you
No day be grievous to you.
Love of each face be yours

A bright flame before thee
A guiding star above thee
A smooth path below thee

Today, tonight and for evermore.

(Adapted from the *Carmina Gadelica*)

THEMED WEDDINGS

Not everyone wants to dress up in the traditional white
dress, top hat and tails. Themed weddings are growing
in popularity and provide a very striking option – if you're
going to dress up you might as well do it in style, though
you may not want to go as far as the couple who married
in the costumes of *Dangerous Liaisons*! A couple in York-
shire recently celebrated their marriage with everyone,
including the vicar, in full Victorian costume. The entire
village apparently entered into the spirit of the occasion.
Another attractive option is to have a 1920s wedding,
with beaded flapper dresses, vintage automobiles, and
Gershwin or Scott Joplin music. There are one or two
wonderful art deco hotels in Britain which are perfect for
it. One of them, on Burgh Island in Devon, has close
associations with Agatha Christie. Following the trend

91

in historical costume drama, a Jane Austen theme would suit an eighteenth-century stately home location and many of them are now licensed for weddings. Costumes and a suitable horse and carriage are very easy to hire.

Many medieval castles are licensed to hold wedding ceremonies and will put on a seventeenth-century banquet. Some will even provide pavilions in the grounds, stage a joust for you, and follow it up with Elizabethan music and dancing. John, a history lecturer, was recently married in full armour, having arrived at the church on a horse! His bride, Aileen, wore a medieval 'Guinevere' dress in embroidered red velvet and a tall, conical headdress and veil. Ancient monuments also provide the perfect setting for Gothic weddings. Choices range from historic venues such as Herstmonceux Castle, Bamburgh Castle (believed to be King Arthur's Joyous Guard), Alnwick Castle (where Harry Potter was filmed) to the ducal magnificence of Blenheim Palace and Syon Park. If your taste is less conventional, the *Directory of Venues* (see Useful Publications) offers a number of unusual locations including the three-masted HMS *Warrior*, moored at Portsmouth, Chester Zoo, Manchester United Football Club, St Bartholomew's Hospital, Haynes Motor Museum and, for film buffs, Pinewood Studios. For a more complete list contact the Registrar General, your local register office or go to **www.theweddingdirectory.co.uk** on the internet.

One couple recently chose to have a Viking wedding – complete with horned helmets – which included a group tour of York Viking Centre for the guests as part of the festivities. A steam engine enthusiast was married on the footplate of a locomotive he had been helping to restore and the reception was held in a series of Pullman carriages while the train steamed gently through the countryside. Everyone entered into the spirit of the occasion and dressed accordingly.

If you like ships but getting married afloat isn't practical, the SS *Great Britain* – Brunel's historic passenger liner, now fully restored and moored in Bristol docks – will host your wedding in turn-of-the-century paddle-steamer style. And, though it's still not possible to get married under sail in British waters, you could hire a three-masted schooner or tea clipper complete with crew and have a ceremony followed by a party on board. In Scotland it will be legal provided you have a registered celebrant and the boat is moored at the time.

If this isn't your style and you've always yearned to go to Barbados for your wedding but can't afford it, arrange your own carnival and hire a steel band to dance to. Other suggestions from America include *Gone with the Wind*, *Star Trek*, *Space Odyssey* and *Rocky Horror* weddings. Forties Hollywood with an eighteen-piece Big Band and a pink Cadillac is also popular and one couple even had a gangster marriage (though without the guns!). For those who fantasize about a toon-town marriage, Disneyworld offer weddings where you can dress up as Disney characters and be Snow White or Cinderella for the day.

ENGINEERS OF THE IMAGINATION

If you want a spectacularly different wedding, this might be just what you need! This unique organization, run by John Fox and Sue Gill, has been designing 'rites of passage' ceremonies for more than twenty-five years. Their intention is 'to create a space where people can hold their own secular ceremonies to mark occasions which are significant in their lives'. They started out as a company of artists, performers and musicians called Welfare State International, staging large-scale celebratory events all over the world, such as lantern festivals, street carnivals and an annual water-side spectacular in northern England with fireworks, blazing boats and flying fish. They were soon being approached to design and stage more personal ceremonies for people who wanted something totally different. They will undertake any aspect of a wedding ceremony, from writing the script to commissioning artwork and arranging music. They will stage-manage the whole thing if you want them to and are also willing to act in an advisory capacity – whether you want a large wedding, or just a small personal ceremony.

Music

Music is a very special part of any wedding ceremony, although it is not obligatory. You may want to choose music from many different moods – quiet background music while the guests are coming in and sitting down, a more dramatic piece as the bride and groom enter and walk towards the celebrant, particular set-pieces at different points in the ceremony, and rousing, celebratory music as the bride and groom walk out together after they are married. If you are using recorded music, you will need to time the pieces beforehand to make sure they are long enough, and have someone to operate the equipment.

Churches and chapels often have a resident organist or pianist who will play for the ceremony, and sometimes there is also a choir. It is customary to pay the choir and the organist – you can discuss their fees with the minister. If you want live music and would like to provide your own musicians you will need to talk to the minister and get his approval. Information on how to find and book musicians can be obtained from the Musicians' Union (see Useful Addresses). If you are having a civil marriage, you will need to talk to whoever is in charge of the venue. The building may need to have a music licence for musicians to perform, although hotels and public halls usually have one. If it is an open-air ceremony you may have to check that everyone will be able to hear the music in the location you have chosen. For outdoor amplified music there are regulations that must be complied with – check with your local environmental health officer.

If you are getting married in a church which has a full peal of bells, you may be able to pay for bell-ringers to ring a celebratory peal. Unfortunately, many churches now have only one bell and some can offer only a recording.

CLASSICAL MUSIC

There are a number of compilations available in the shops, including the Classical Moods collection and a selection of romantic classics from Past Times.

Handel: Arrival of the Queen of Sheba (*Solomon*)
            Music for the Royal Fireworks

Let the Bright Seraphim
Hallelujah Chorus

Vivaldi: Gloria (Gloria in D, RV 589)

Purcell: Trumpet Tune and Air

Predieri: Pace una volta (from *Zenobia*), versions for organ, trumpet and voice

Bach: Prelude and Fugue in G 'The Great'
Jesu Joy of Man's Desiring

Jeremiah Clarke: Trumpet Voluntary

Vidor: Toccata (Symphony No. 5 in F Major Op. 42)

Beethoven: Ode to Joy (Symphony No. 9)

Tchaikovsky: 1812 Overture

Mendelssohn: Wedding March

Ninth-century Bells and Airs by Fingal ('Scotland's Music', Linn Records)

Vaughan Williams: Greensleeves

Wagner: Bridal March (*Lohengrin*)

Coleridge Taylor: Hiawatha's Wedding

Jan Gabarek: Officium (solo saxophone and Gregorian chant)

Mozart: Piano Concerto No. 21 'Elvira Madigan'
Ave Maria

Canteloube: Chants d'Auvergne (Songs from the Auvergne)

O'Carolan's Receipt (eighteenth-century Irish harp music)

MODERN MUSIC

There are numerous compilation albums of romantic music. Everyone will have their own favourites – these are taken from the top hundred most popular love songs played at civil weddings.

'It's Got to be Perfect', Fairground Attraction
'And I Love You So', Don MacLean
'Annie's Song', John Denver
'River Deep, Mountain High', Ike and Tina Turner
'More than Words', Extreme
'State of Independence', Donna Summer
'Ain't No Stoppin' Us Now', Enigma
'You've Got a Friend', Carole King
'I Will Always Love You', Whitney Houston
'You are the Wind Beneath my Wings', Whitney Houston/Bette Midler
'Stairway to Heaven', Far Corporation; Eric Clapton; various
'True Love', Bing Crosby and Grace Kelly (from the film *High Society*)
'A Groovy Kind of Love', Phil Collins; Simon and Garfunkel
'You Look Wonderful Tonight', Eric Clapton
'Everything I Do, I Do for You', Bryan Adams
'When a Man Loves a Woman', Percy Sledge

'Sweet Dreams', Eurythmics

'Right By Your Side', Eurythmics

'The Miracle of Love', Eurythmics

'There Must Be an Angel', Eurythmics

'How Deep is the Ocean', Frank Sinatra; various

'Stand By Me', Ben E. King

'Dedicated to the One I Love', Shirelles; Mamas and Papas; various

'Misty', Johnny Mathis

'Trust in Me', Etta James

'Every Breath You Take', Police

'Love is a Many Splendoured Thing', Sinatra; various

'Always on My Mind', Elvis Presley

'Love me Tender', Elvis Presley

'Evergreen', Barbara Streisand/Will Young

'My Only Love', Neil Diamond

'I'll Have to Say I Love You in a Song', Jim Croce

'Paradise', Nat King Cole

'The Only One', Lionel Richie

'Song for Guy', Elton John

'Your Song', Elton John

'We've Only Just Begun', Carpenters

'I'm on the Top of the World', Carpenters

'Waiting for a Girl like You', Foreigner

'Up Where We Belong', Julie Warne and Joe Cocker

'Kiss You All Over', Exiles

'All I Ask of You', from *Phantom of the Opera*

'Imagine', John Lennon

'The Look of Love', Dusty Springfield

'My Heart Will Go On', Celine Dion

'Fields of Gold', Eva Cassidy/Sting

'Tonight I Celebrate my Love for You', Peabo Bryson
and Roberta Flack

'Woman', John Lennon

'Close to You', The Carpenters

'When I'm Sixty Four', The Beatles

JAZZ/SWING

'Triple Celebration', Stan Tracey Quintet

'Moonlight Serenade', Glenn Miller

'String of Pearls'

'Amazing Grace' (traditional)

'When the Saints Go Marching In'

'It's a Wonderful World', Louis Armstrong

Epilogue

RENEWAL OF VOWS

The Church of Scotland Common Order Book has a ceremony of Thanksgiving for Marriage, to be used on an anniversary, or after 'a time of separation, or when a couple has experienced difficulty in their marriage'. This ceremony includes the renewal of marriage vows.

Anne and Andrew, who married in England and then went to live in America, recently celebrated their twenty-fifth wedding anniversary by renewing their vows in the village church where the original ceremony was held. The vicar conducted a private service in front of close family members and a small number of guests, some of whom had been present at the wedding. He made a short speech on the subject of marriage and Anne and Andrew repeated their vows with slightly altered wording, adding a few lines thanking each other for their love, friendship and tolerance through twenty-five years of living together. Two of their children read the passage on love from 1 Corinthians, chapter 13 and Kuan Tao-Sheng's poem 'Married Love' (see the Anthology of Readings).

A RITUAL TO MARK DIVORCE

Divorce is a public acknowledgment of the death of a relationship. It is as important to recognize and mourn divorce as it is to celebrate marriage. Divorce is a threshold between one part of your life and another. Many second partnerships fail because of the weight of emotional luggage brought into them from previous relationships. A ritual which helps partners to work through this and which marks a symbolic end to this period of their lives together can be tremendously valuable.

Lorna St Aubyn, in *Rituals for Everyday Living*, constructs a ceremony for divorce which involves 'undoing' the original marriage vows and a dialogue which honestly tries to analyse why they were not kept. The book stresses that 'feelings of resentment and hatred are as binding and powerful as those of love, and self-forgiveness is as important as the forgiving of others'. The end of the ritual is positive, stressing the good things that have come from the relationship. Even if it ended acrimoniously, she writes, 'the time and love you invested in it were not wasted. By thanking each other for what the association brought you, that gift of yourselves is validated. Where the relationship ended by mutual consent because its life force had been expended, the giving of thanks is also helpful because it acknowledges the need to seal off a completed cycle. Through understanding how it has enriched you, you can make full use of it and carry into the next cycle only what will be helpful.'

Under the new legislation, many divorces now are uncontested and may not even necessitate an appearance in court. The decree nisi is read out before the court without either partner having to be there. Six weeks later a piece of paper arrives through the letter-box which tells you that your marriage is over and it can seem very unreal. Even the simple act of going to court to hear the declaration read can be immensely valuable.

Steve and Megan, both in their thirties and working in financial services, divorced amicably after six years of marriage. 'There wasn't anything left between us,' Megan said. 'We bored each other.' During the two-year separation period they remained friends and occasionally met for a drink after work. They also kept contact with their in-laws who continued to treat them as if nothing had happened. The decree absolute arrived one morning in the post but nothing really changed. 'I always had the nagging feeling I was still married,' Steve told me. 'Even though we had the bit of paper that said we weren't!'

Eventually they organized a party in the function room of a local pub and invited all the friends and relatives who had come to their wedding. After everyone had arrived and had a few drinks, Steve's brother Mike, who had been their best man, called for silence and made a short speech. Steve and Megan then made a statement, explaining why they had decided to get divorced, expressing regret that their marriage hadn't worked, and asking all their friends and relatives to continue to support them in their single lives. They turned to each other, clasped hands and then each made the following statement to the other: 'I, Megan, willingly release you, Steve, from your marriage vows and declare that you are now free to live as you please, with whoever you please. I hope that we will always remain friends and I wish you all the best for the future.'

Mike then separated their hands and formally declared their marriage at an end. Steve and Megan put a match to a copy of their marriage certificate and watched it burn to ashes on a metal tray. Then they popped the champagne corks.

'I felt really sad,' Megan said. 'It was the first time it really hit me.'

Bani Shorter, in her book *An Image Darkly Forming*, describes the experience of Nicole, a gifted musician whose marriage failed and who was faced with the loss, not only of the relationship, but of the dream home they had created together. She was so depressed that she found herself unable to play. Counselling helped her to come to terms with the break-up of her marriage, but the final trauma of moving out of the house had to be dealt with in a very special way.

Nicole created a ritual, allowing herself three days to clean the house, tidy the garden, say goodbye to every room. She slept in the house alone. At the end of the three days she went out 'and gathered flowers from the garden, brought them in and arranged them in all her favourite places. The house was beautiful, she said. She then bathed and dressed and packed her bag. But, before she left, during the long twilight of the still evening, she took her instrument from the case, lifted her fingers and played a recital of favourite pieces. When she closed the door at last, she put her key through the letter-box, leaving the home-no-longer-hers behind forever.' Nicole had conducted a kind of funeral rite for the death of her relationship and the romantic fantasy that the house had represented. As a consequence she was able to move forward constructively to a new stage of her life.

Linda, a forty-three-year-old mother with two grown-up children, found herself at the end of a destructive relationship, unable to break free from it and move on. Despite a lengthy period of counselling, she still had lurid dreams, a constant feeling of anxiety and moments when she felt in danger of being dragged back into the destructive spiral. Her obsession with her previous partner was also preventing her from making a new relationship.

With a few friends she devised a ceremony. First of all they spent a couple of hours on a ruthless spring clean, collecting together everything that had belonged to Linda's partner or had strong associations. Then candles were lit around the room. Letters and objects from the relationship were read and wept over and placed in a box tied with strong cord to keep in the dark forces Linda somehow believed were associated with them. A dummy figure, like a Guy Fawkes doll, was dressed in old clothes that had belonged to her partner.

Friends then symbolically tied Linda to the dummy with a length of cord, placing the box between them. Linda faced the dummy and made a speech telling it how she felt and that the relationship was now over. She made a declaration to her friends that she was leaving the past behind and moving forward, asking them to pledge their support. This they promised to do. Her friends then cut the cord with a pair of scissors.

For Linda to feel completely released, there had to be one more stage. She picked up the box and both it and the guy figure were burnt on a bonfire in the garden (if this is too gruesome, the guy could just as easily be dismantled and its components put in the trash – the clothes perhaps given to Oxfam). Linda and her friends then had a celebration with wine and food.

She is coping with life much better now and has a new partner.

Anthology of Readings, Blessings and Poems

NEVER MARRY BUT FOR LOVE

Never marry but for love; but see that thou lovest what is lovely. He that minds a body and not a soul has not the better part of that relation, and will consequently lack the noblest comfort of a married life.

Between a man and his wife nothing ought to rule but love . . . As love ought to bring them together, so it is the best way to keep them well together. A husband and wife that love one another show their children . . . that they should do so too. Others visibly lose their authority in their families by their contempt of one another; and teach their children to be unnatural by their own examples.

Let not enjoyment lessen, but augment, affection; it being the basest of passions to like when we have not, what we slight when we possess. Here it is we ought to search out our pleasure, where the field is large and full of variety, and of an enduring nature; sickness, poverty or disgrace being not able to shake it because it is not under the moving influences of worldly contingencies.

Nothing can be more entire and without reserve; nothing more zealous, affectionate and sincere; nothing more contented and constant than such a couple, nor greater temporal felicity than to be one of them.

William Penn

CELTIC BLESSING

May the God of peace guard
The door of your house,
The door of your heart.
May the road rise to meet you,
And the sun stand at your shoulder.
May the wind be always at your back,
And the rains fall softly upon your fields.
May life itself befriend you
Each day, each night,
Each step of your journey.

May the peace of the spirit be with you
And with your children,
From the day that we have here today-
To the day of the end of your lives,
Until the day of the end of your lives

THIS DAY

Look to this day! For it is life, the very life of life. In its brief course lie all the varieties and realities of your existence; the bliss of growth, the glory of action, the splendour of beauty. For yesterday is already a dream, and tomorrow is only a vision, but today, well lived, makes every yesterday a dream of happiness, and every tomorrow a vision of hope.

Look well, therefore, to this day! Such is the salutation of the dawn.

From the Sanskrit

HE WISHES FOR THE CLOTHS OF HEAVEN

Had I the heavens' embroidered cloths,
Enwrought with golden and silver light,
The blue and the dim and the dark cloths
Of night and light and the half-light,
I would spread the cloths under your feet;
But I, being poor, have only my dreams;
I have spread my dreams under your feet;
Tread softly because you tread on my dreams.

W.B. Yeats

LOVE

Though I speak with tongues of men and of angels, and have not Love I am become as sounding brass, or a tinkling cymbal. And though I have the gift of prophecy and understand all mysteries and all knowledge; and though I have all faith, so that I could remove mountains and have not Love I am nothing, and though I bestow all my goods to feed the poor and though I give my body to be burned and have not Love it profiteth me nothing.

Love suffereth long and is kind; Love envieth not; Love vaunteth not itself, is not puffed up; doth not behave itself unseemly, seeketh not her own, is not easily provoked, thinketh no evil; rejoiceth not in iniquity, but rejoiceth in the truth; beareth all things, believeth all things, hopeth all things, endureth all things.

Love never faileth; but whether there be prophecies, they shall fail; whether there be tongues, they shall cease; whether there be knowledge, it shall vanish away. For we know imperfectly and we prophesy imperfectly. But when that which is perfect is come, then that which is imperfect shall be done away.

When I was a child, I spake as a child, I understood as a child, I thought as a child; but when I became a man, I put away childish things. For now we see through glass, darkly, but then face to face; now I know imperfectly, but then shall I know even as also I am known. And now abideth Faith, Hope and Love – these three; but the greatest of these is Love.

1 Corinthians, chapter 13

LOVE LIES BEYOND THE TOMB

Love lies beyond
The tomb, the earth, which fades like dew!
I love the fond,
The faithful, and the true.

Love lies in sleep,
The happiness of healthy dreams:
Eve's dews may weep,
But love delightful seems.

'Tis seen in flowers,
And in the even's pearly dew;
On the earth's green hours,
And in the heaven's eternal blue.

'Tis heard in spring
When light and sunbeams, warm and kind,
On angel's wing
Bring love and music to the mind.

And where is voice,
So young, so beautifully sweet
As nature's choice,
When spring and lovers meet?

Love lies beyond
The tomb, the earth, the flowers, and dew.
I love the fond,
The faithful, young and true.

John Clare

LOVE'S EXCHANGE

My true love hath my heart, and I have his,
By just exchange, one for the other given.
I hold his dear, and mine he cannot miss:
There never was a better bargain driven.
His heart in me, keeps me and him in one,
My heart in him, his thoughts and senses guides:
He loves my heart, for once it was his own:
I cherish his, because in me it bides.
His heart his wound received from my sight:
My heart was wounded with his wounded heart,
For as from me, on him his hurt did light,
So still methought in me his hurt did smart:
    Both equal hurt, in this change sought our bliss:
    My true love hath my heart and I have his.

Sir Philip Sidney

From THE SONG OF SOLOMON

My beloved spake and said unto me, rise up, my love, my fair one, and come away,

For Lo, the winter is past, the rain is over and gone;

The flowers appear on the earth; the time of the singing of birds is come, and the voice of the turtle is heard in our land;

The fig tree putteth forth her green figs, and the vines with the tender grape give a good smell, Arise, my love, my fair one, and come away.

Oh my dove, thou art in the clefts of the rock, in the secret places of the stairs, let me see thy countenance, let me hear thy voice; for sweet is thy voice, and thy countenance is comely.

My beloved is mine and I am his; he feedeth among the lilies.

Until the day break and the shadows flee away, turn my beloved, and be thou like a roe or a young hart upon the mountains . . .

Set me as a seal upon thine heart, as a seal upon thine arm: for love is strong as death;

Many waters cannot quench love, neither can the floods drown it.

SONG

Love and harmony combine,
And around our souls entwine
While thy branches mix with mine,
And our roots together join.

Joy upon our branches sit,
Chirping loud and singing sweet;
Like gentle streams beneath our feet
Innocence and virtue meet.

Thou the golden fruit dost bear,
I am clad in flowers fair;
Thy sweet boughs perfume the air,
And the turtle buildeth there.

There she sits and feeds her young,
Sweet I hear her mournful song;
And thy lovely leaves among,
There is love, I hear his tongue.

There his charming nest doth lay,
There he sleeps the night away;
There he sports along the day,
And doth among our branches play.

William Blake

COMMITMENT

Ultimately there comes a time when a decision must be made. Ultimately two people who love each other must ask themselves how much they hope for as their love grows and deepens, and how much risk they are willing to take. It is indeed a fearful gamble. Because it is the nature of love to create, a marriage itself is something which has to be created.

To marry is the biggest risk in human relations that a person can take. If we commit ourselves to one person for life this is not, as many people think, a rejection of freedom; rather it demands the courage to move into all the risks of freedom and the risk of love which is permanent; into that love which is not possession but participation. It takes a lifetime to learn another person.

When love is not possession, but participation, then it is part of that co-creation which is our human calling.

Madeleine L'Engle, The Irrational Season

FROM A NATIVE AMERICAN CEREMONY

May the sun bring you new strength by day;
May the moon softly restore you by night.
May the rain wash away your fears
And the breeze invigorate your being.
May you, all the days of your life,

Walk gently through the world
And know its beauty.

Now you will feel no rain, for each will shelter the other.
Now you will feel no cold, for each will warm the other.
Now you will feel no solitude, for each will company the
    other.
Now you are two persons, but both will lead one life.
Go now to your dwelling to begin the days of your life
    together,
And may your days be good and long upon the earth.

THE PROS AND CONS

'Tis a hazard both ways I confess, to live single or to
marry . . . It may be bad, it may be good, as it is a cross
and calamity on the one side, so 'tis a sweet delight, an
incomparable happiness, a blessed estate, a most
unspeakable benefit, a sole content, on the other, 'tis all
in the proof. Be not then so wayward, so covetous, so
distrustful, so curious and nice, but let's all marry!

Robert Burton, The Anatomy of Melancholy

A BIRTHDAY

My heart is like a singing bird
    Whose nest is in a watered shoot;
My heart is like an apple-tree

Whose boughs are bent with thickset fruit;
My heart is like a rainbow shell
    That paddles in a halcyon sea;
My heart is gladder than all these
    Because my love is come to me.

Raise me a dais of silk and down;
    Hang it with vair and purple dyes;
Carve it in doves and pomegranates,
    And peacocks with a hundred eyes;
Work it in gold and silver grapes,
    In leaves and silver fleurs-de-lys;
Because the birthday of my life
    Is come, my love is come to me.

Christina Rossetti

COMMITMENT

Wherever you go, I will go;
And wherever you stay, I will stay;
Your people shall be my people,
And your God, my God.
Where you die, I will also die,
And there will I be buried with you.
May nothing but death part us
By God's help.

Ruth's commitment to Naomi, Old Testament, Ruth: Chapter 1, verses 16–17

In this place, in this period of quietness, let us all think for a moment of [name] and [name]. This is a new beginning for them, with all their hopes and dreams of love. May these hopes and dreams be realized. May they believe in each other; May they be devoted to each other; May the warmth of their love for each other, in the kindness of their home, allow them to be charitable to others as well as to themselves. Through their years together, may their love grow and deepen through giving, each to the other. May they learn the great joy that comes from sharing.

From the Jewish marriage ceremony (freely adapted)

TO MY DEAR AND LOVING HUSBAND

If ever two were one, then surely we.
If ever man were loved by wife, then thee;
If ever wife was happy in a man,
Compare with me ye women if you can.
I prize thy love more than whole mines of gold,
Or all the riches that the East doth hold.
My love is such that river cannot quench,
Nor aught but love from thee, give recompence.
Thy love is such I can no way repay,
The heavens reward thee manifold I pray.
Then while we live, in love lets so persever,
That when we love no more, we may live ever.

Anne Bradstreet

So ancient is the desire of one another which is implanted in us, reuniting our original nature, seeking to make one of two, and to heal the state of man. Each of us when separated, having one side only, like a flat fish, is but the tally-half of a man, and he is always looking for his other half . . . There is not a man . . . who would not acknowledge that this meeting and melting into one another, this becoming one instead of two, was the very expression of his ancient need. And the reason is that human nature was originally one and we were a whole, and the desire and pursuit of the whole is called Love.

Plato, The Symposium

THE UNION OF YOU AND ME

It is for the union of you and me
that there is light in the sky.
It is for the union of you and me
that the earth is decked in dusky green.

It is for the union of you and me
that night sits motionless with the world in her arms;
dawn appears opening the eastern door
with sweet murmurs in her voice.

The boat of hope sails along on the currents of
eternity towards that union,
flowers of the age are being gathered together
for its welcoming ritual.

It is for the union of you and me
that this heart of mine, in the garb of a bride,
has proceeded from birth to birth
upon the surface of this ever-turning world
to choose the beloved.

Rabindranath Tagore

THE GOOD MORROW

I wonder by my troth, what thou and I
    Did, till we loved? were we not weaned till then?
But sucked on country pleasures, childishly?
    Or snorted we i'the seven sleepers' den?
'Twas so: But this, all pleasures fancies be.
If ever any beauty I did see,
Which I desired and got, 'twas but a dream of thee.
    And now good morrow to our waking souls,
    Which watch not one another out of fear;
For love, all love of other sights controls,
    And makes one little room, an everywhere.
Let sea-discoverers to new worlds have gone,
Let maps to others, worlds on worlds have shown,
Let us possess our world, each hath one, and is one.

My face in thine eye, thine in mine appears,
  And true plain hearts do in the faces rest,
Where can we find two better hemispheres
  Without sharp North, without declining West?
  Whatever dies, was not mixed equally;
  If our two loves be one, or, thou and I
Love so alike, that none do slacken, none can die.

John Donne

AT THE WEDDING MARCH

God with honour hang your head,
Groom, and grace you, bride, your bed
With lissome scions, sweet scions,
Out of hallowed bodies bred.

Each be other's comfort kind;
Deep, deeper than divined,
Divine charity, dear charity,
Fast you ever, fast bind.

Then let the March tread our ears;
I to him turn with tears
Who to wedlock, his wonder wedlock,
Deals triumph and immortal years.

Gerard Manley Hopkins

THOUGHTS ON MARRIAGE

What could be more sweet than to live with one to whom you are united in body and mind, who talks with you in secret affection, and to whom you have committed all your faith and your fortune? What in all nature is lovelier? You are bound to friends in affection. How much more are you bound to a husband or wife in the highest love, with union of the body, the bond of mutual vows and the sharing of your property! . . . Nothing is more safe, tranquil, pleasant and loving than marriage.

Erasmus

HOW DO I LOVE THEE

How do I love thee? Let me count the ways.
    I love thee to the depth and breadth and height
My soul can reach, when feeling out of sight
    For the ends of Being and ideal Grace.
I love thee to the level of everyday's
    Most quiet need, by sun and candle-light.
I love thee freely, as men strive for Right;
    I love thee purely, as they turn from Praise.
I love thee with the passion put to use
    In my old griefs, and with my childhood's faith.
I love thee with a love I seemed to lose

With my lost saints – I love thee with the breath,
Smiles, tears, of all my life! – and if God choose,
I shall but love thee better after death.

Elizabeth Barrett Browning

Lovers or friends desire two things. The one is to love each other so much that they enter into each other and only make one being. The other is to love each other so much that, having half the globe between them, their union will not be diminished in the slightest degree. All any human being desires here below is perfectly realised in God. We have all these impossible desires within us as a mark of our destination.

The love between God and God, which in itself is God, is this bond of double virtue; the bond which unites two beings so closely that they are no longer distinguishable and really form a single unity, and the bond which stretches across distance and triumphs over infinite separation.

It is only necessary to know that love is a direction and not a state of the soul.

Simone Weil, Waiting for God

THE PASSIONATE SHEPHERD TO HIS LOVE

Come live with me and be my Love,
And we will all the pleasures prove
That hills and valleys, dales and fields,
Or woods or steepy mountains yields.

And we will sit upon the rocks,
And see the shepherds feed their flocks
By shallow rivers, to whose falls
Melodious birds sing madrigals.

And I will make thee beds of roses
And a thousand fragrant posies;
A cap of flowers, and a kirtle
Embroidered all with leaves of myrtle.

A gown made of the finest wool
Which from our pretty lambs we pull;
Fair-lined slippers for the cold,
With buckles of the purest gold.

A belt of straw and ivy-buds
With coral clasps and amber studs:
And if these pleasures may thee move,
Come live with me and be my Love.

The shepherd swains shall dance and sing
For thy delight each May morning:

If these delights thy mind may move,
Then live with me and be my Love.

Christopher Marlowe

FOR BETTER, FOR WORSE

It is not enough to love passionately: you must also love
well. A passionate love is good doubtless, but a beautiful
love is better. May you have as much strength as gentle-
ness; may it lack nothing, not even forbearance, and let
even a little compassion be mingled with it . . . you are
human and, because of this, capable of much suffering.
If then something of compassion does not enter into the
feelings you have one for the other, these feelings will
not always befit all the circumstances of your life
together; they will be like festive robes that will not shield
you from wind and rain. We love truly only those we
love even in their weakness and their poverty. To forbear,
to forgive, to console – that alone is the science of love.

Anatole France

THE CONFIRMATION

Yes, yours, my love, is the right human face.
I in my mind had waited for this long,
Seeing the false and searching for the true,
Then found you as a traveller finds a place

Of welcome suddenly amid the wrong
Valleys and rocks and twisting roads. But you,
What shall I call you? A fountain in a waste,
A well of water in a country dry,
Or anything that's honest and good, an eye
That makes the whole world bright. Your open heart,
Simple with giving, gives the primal deed,
The first good world, the blossom, the blowing seed,
The hearth, the steadfast land, the wandering sea,
Not beautiful or rare in every part,
But like yourself, as they were meant to be.

Edwin Muir

THE DANCE

A good relationship has a pattern like a dance, and is
built on some of the same rules. The partners do not
need to hold on tightly, because they move confidently
in the same pattern, intricate but gay, and swift and free,
like a country dance of Mozart's. To touch heavily would
be to arrest the pattern and freeze the movement, to
check the endlessly changing beauty of its unfolding.
There is no place here for the possessive clutch, the cling-
ing arm, the heavy hand; only the barest touch in pass-
ing. Now arm in arm, now face to face, now back to
back – it does not matter which. Because they know
they are partners moving to the same rhythm, creating
a pattern together, and being invisibly nourished by it.

The joy of such a pattern is not only the joy of creation or the joy of participation, it is also the joy of living in the moment. Lightness of touch and living in the moment are intertwined.

Anne Morrow Lindbergh, A Gift from the Sea

SONNET

Let me not to the marriage of true minds
    Admit impediments. Love is not love
Which alters when it alteration finds.
    Nor bends with the remover to remove:
O, no! it is an ever-fixed mark,
    That looks on tempests and is never shaken;
It is the star to every wandering bark,
    Whose worth's unknown, although his height be taken.

Love's not Time's fool, though rosy lips and cheeks
    Within his bending sickle's compass come;
    Love alters not with his brief hours and weeks,
But bears it out even to the edge of doom.
    If this be error and upon me proved,
    I never writ, nor no man ever loved.

William Shakespeare

MARRIAGE IS ONE LONG CONVERSATION

Marriage is one long conversation, chequered by disputes. The disputes are valueless; they but ingrain the difference; the heroic heart of woman prompting her at once to nail her colours to the mast. But in the intervals, almost unconsciously, and with no desire to shine, the whole material of life is turned over and over, ideas are struck out and shared, the two persons more and more adapt their notions one to suit the other, and in process of time, without sound of trumpet, they conduct each other into new worlds of thought.

Robert Louis Stevenson

MARRIED LOVE

You and I
Have so much love,
That it
Burns like fire,
In which we bake a lump of clay
Moulded into a figure of you
And a figure of me.
Then we take both of them,
And break them into pieces,
And mix the pieces with water,
And mould again a figure of you,

And a figure of me.
I am in your clay.
You are in my clay.
In life we share a single quilt,
In death we will share one coffin.

Kuan Tao-Sheng

MARRIAGE

Then Almitra spoke again and said, And what of
    Marriage, master?
And he answered saying:
You were born together, and together you shall be for
    evermore.
You shall be together when the white wings of death
    scatter your days.
Aye, you shall be together even in the silent memory
    of God.
But let there be spaces in your togetherness.
And let the winds of the heavens dance between you.

Love one another, but make not a bond of love;
Let it rather be a moving sea between the shores of
    your souls.
Fill each other's cup but drink not from one cup.
Give one another of your bread but eat not from the
    same loaf.

Sing and dance together and be joyous, but let each
    one of you be alone,
Even as the strings of a lute are alone though they
    quiver with the same music.

Give your hearts, but not into each other's keeping.
For only the hand of Life can contain your hearts.
And stand together yet not too near together;
For the pillars of the temple stand apart,
And the oak tree and the cypress grow not in each
    other's shadow.

Kahlil Gibran, The Prophet

PERFECT LOVE

O perfect Love, all human thought transcending,
Lowly we kneel in prayer before your throne,
That you will give the love which knows no ending,
To those whom evermore you join in one.

O perfect Love, become their full assurance,
Of tender love and steadfast godly faith;
Of patient hope, and quiet brave endurance,
With childlike trust that fears not pain or death.

Grant them the joy that lightens earthly sorrow,
Grant them the peace that calms all earthly strife,

And to life's day the glorious bright tomorrow
That dawns upon eternal love and life.

Dorothy Gurney
(*For a musical setting, see the Methodist Hymn Book*)

THE NATURE OF LOVE

Beloved, let us love one another: for love is of God; and every one that loveth is born of God, and knoweth God. He that loveth not knoweth not God; for God is love.
In this was manifested the love of God toward us, because that God sent his only begotten Son into the world, that we might live through him.
Herein is love, not that we loved God, but that he loved us, and sent his Son to be the propitiation for our sins.
Beloved, if God so loved us, we ought also to love one another.
No man hath seen God at any time. If we love one another God dwelleth in us, and his love is perfected in us . . .
Herein is our love made perfect, that we may have boldness in the day of judgement; because as he is, so are we in this world.
There is no fear in love; but perfect love casteth out fear; because fear hath torment. He that feareth is not made perfect in love.
We love him, because he first loved us.

If a man say, I love God, and hateth his brother, he is a liar; for he that loveth not his brother whom he hath seen, how can he love God whom he hath not seen? And this commandment have we from him, that he who loveth God love his brother also.

First Epistle of John, Chapter 4, verses 7–21

SONNET

Shall I compare thee to a summer's day?
   Thou art more lovely and more temperate:
Rough winds do shake the darling buds of May,
   And summer's lease hath all too short a date:
Sometime too hot the eye of heaven shines,
   And often is his gold complexion dimmed;
And every fair from fair sometimes declines,
   By chance, or nature's changing course untrimmed;
But thy eternal summer shall not fade,
   Nor lose possession of that fair thou owest,
Nor shall death brag thou wanderest in his shade,
   When in eternal lines to time thou growest;
   So long as men can breathe, or eyes can see,
   So long lives this, and this gives life to thee.

William Shakespeare

EPITHALAMIUM

Open the temple gates unto my love,
Open them wide that she may enter in,
And all the posts adorn as doth behove,
And all the pillars deck with garlands trim,
For to receive this Saint with honour due
That cometh in to you . . .

Bring her up to th'high altar, that she may
The sacred ceremonies there partake
The which do endless Matrimony make,
And let the roaring Organs loudly play
The praises of the Lord in lively notes,
The whiles with hollow throats
The Choristers the joyous Anthem sing,
That all the woods may answer and their echo ring.

Now all is done; bring home the bride again,
Bring home the triumph of our victory,
Bring home with you the glory of her gain,
With joyance bring her and with jollity.
Never had man more joyfull day than this,
Whom heaven would heap with bliss.
Make feast therefore now all this live long day,
This day for ever to me holy is,
Pour out the wine without restraint or stay . . .

Crown ye God Bacchus with a coronall,
And Hymen also crown with wreaths of vine,
And let the Graces dance unto the rest;
For they can do it best:
The whiles the maidens do their carol sing,
To which the woods shall answer and their echo ring.

Edmund Spenser

Useful Publications

Boswell, John, *The Marriage of Likeness: Same-Sex Unions*, HarperCollins, 1995

Butler, Becky, *Ceremonies of the Heart (An Anthology of Lesbian Unions)*, Seal Press, 1990

Carr-Gomm, Philip, *The Druid Way*, Element, 1993

Directory of Venues Licensed for Civil Marriage, The Registrar General, General Register Office (see Useful Addresses)

Cault, Tony and Baz Kershaw (eds), *Engineers of the Imagination*, rev. edn Methuen, 1990

Gillies, Midge, *The Wedding Book*, Bloomsbury, 1997

Lacey, Richard, *Hard to Swallow: A Brief History of Food*, CUP, 1994

Perry, Rev. Michael and Rowena Edlin-White, *Design

Your Own Wedding Ceremony, Marshall Pickering, 1997

Rayner, Rabbi John D., *A Guide to Jewish Marriage*, Union of Liberal and Progressive Synagogues (see Useful Addresses)

Ross-Macdonald, Jane, *Alternative Weddings*, Thomsons, 1996

Rubinstein Helge (ed.), *The Oxford Book of Marriage*, OUP, 1990

St Aubyn, Lorna, *Rituals for Everyday Living*, Piatkus, 1994

Stallworthy, Jon (ed.), *Penguin Book of Love Poetry*, 1976

Toussaint-Samat, Maguelonne, *A History of Food*, Blackwell, 1994

Ward and Wild, *Human Rites*, Mowbray, 1994

Wynne Wilson, Jane, *Sharing the Future: A Practical Guide to Non-Religious Wedding Ceremonies*, 4th edn., The British Humanist Association, 1996

Useful Websites and Addresses

www.statistics.gov.uk/nsbase/registration/ marriage.asp Information on the legal formalities and requirements for marriage in England and Wales.

www.confetti.co.uk

www.weddingdirectory.co.uk

www.wedding-service.co.uk These sites provide a comprehensive guide to everything you need to know about getting married, whatever kind of ceremony you envisage. Lots of useful information and links to other sites. Lists of venues and a comprehensive index of sources to help you find the services you need.

www.world-wedding-traditions.net A guide to marriage customs around the world.

www.interfaithministers.org.uk Interfaith ministers will conduct marriages between partners of different

faiths and offer spiritual counselling to help resolve difficulties. They are also sometimes willing to conduct
alternative ceremonies of partnership and commitment
as well as those between same sex couples.

www.bindibrides.co.uk An excellent site for Asian
brides/grooms, which also has a section on cross-cultural
marriages and a resident agony aunt.

www.weddings-abroad.com A good guide to marrying abroad.

http://speeches.com/open.asp Help with preparing
speeches for the big day. There are ready-made suggestions, or you can customize your own.

**www.netspace.net.au/~afcc/Pages/
MarriageLegal.htm** Information on marriage in Australia for both residents and non-residents.

www.bdm.govt.nz/diawebsite.nsf/ Information on
marriages in New Zealand.

British Buddhist Association, 11 Biddulph Road,
London W9 1JA. Tel. 020 7286 5575.

British Humanist Association, 47 Theobald's Road,
London WCIX 8SP. Tel. 020 7430 0908.

Catholic Marriage Advisory Council, Clitherow
House, 1 Blythe Mews, Brokk Garden, London W14
0NW. Tel. 020 7371 1341.

Disney Weddings, Walt Disney Attractions. Tel. 020
8222 1000.

Dragonpaths, E-mail> annie.dragonpaths@virgin.net

Engineers of the Imagination, The Ellers, Ulverston,
Cumbria, LA12 0AA. Tel. 01229 581127.

info@welfare-state.com

Freelance Celebrant: Rev. Jonathon Blake, an ordained former Church of England minister, believes strongly in separating the legal and spiritual elements of marriage. He helps couples to create a uniquely personal ceremony free from the rules and regulations restricting traditional rites. He conducts both spiritual and civil ceremonies indoors, outdoors and in unusual locations, and will also marry divorcees, inter-faith and same-sex couples. Whispering Trees, 273 Beechings Way, Gillingham, Kent ME8 7BP. Tel. 01634 262920 or 01322 525678.

Historic Scotland, Events Manager, Longmore House, Salisbury Place, Edinburgh, EH9 1SH. Tel. 0131 668 8600.

Jewish Marriage Council, 23 Ravenshurst Avenue, London NW4 4EE. Tel. 020 8203 6311.

Lesbian and Gay Christian Movement, Oxford House, Derbyshire Street, London E2 6HG. Tel. 020 7739 1249.

Metropolitan Community Church, *London*: St Benet's Chapel, 327a Mile End Road, London, E1. E-mail> MCCLondon@compuserve.com
www.mccel.demon.co.uk
Bournemouth: Hannington Road, Potkesdown, Bournemouth, Dorset, BH7 6JT.
www.churchnet.org.uk/ukchurches/metro.shtml
Manchester: P.O. Box 19, M34 3XF. E-mail> revandy@ easynet.co.uk
Worldwide: E-mail> UFmccHq@aol.com
www.mccmanchester.freeserve.co.uk

Musicians' Union, National Office, 60/62 Clapham Road, London SW9 0JJ. Tel. 020 7840 5534.

National Trust for Scotland, 28 Charlotte Square, Edinburgh EH2 4DU. Tel. 0131 243 9300.

Pagan Federation, BM Box 7097, London SC1N 3XX. E-Mail> Secretary@Pagan Fed.demon.co.uk **www.paganfed.co.uk**

Quakers (The Religious Society of Friends), Friends House, 173–177 Euston Road, London NW1 2BJ. Tel. 020 7663 1000.

Registrar General, General Register Office, Smedley Hydro, Trafalgar Road, Berkdale, Southport, PR8 2HH. Tel. 0870 243 7788 **www.statistics.gov.uk/nsbase/ registration/marriage.asp**

Registration Office, Gretna Green, Central Avenue, Gretna, Dumfries & Galloway, Scotland DG16 5AQ. Tel. 01461 337648 **www.gretnaonline.net**

Royal Exchange Costume Hire: National theatrical costumier and private hire for small or large events, has something to suit a variety of budgets. Also willing to make costumes and wedding dresses to order. Anita Quinn, Royal Exchange Costume Hire, 47–53 Swann Street, Manchester, M4 5JY. Tel. 0161 8339333.

Union of Liberal and Progressive Synagogues, The Montagu Centre, 21 Maple Street, London W1P 7DS. Tel. 020 7580 1663.

Unitarian Church, Essex Hall, 1–6 Essex Street, London WC2R 3HY. Tel. 020 7240 2384.

Virgin Snow Weddings, Virgin Holidays Ltd, The

Galleria, Station Road, Crawley, W. Sussex, RH10 1WW. Tel. 0870 9908825. Details on the back of the Virgin Holiday Ski brochures.

Index

Figures in italics indicate illustrations.